ALIGN
LIVING LIFE
ON PURPOSE

JW RUCKER JR, MS.Ed

DEDICATION

To my Mom and Dad for teaching me how to serve others.

To my bride Adrianne for her love wisdom, strength, and her passion for teaching.

To my intelligent and beautiful daughters Yolanda, Naomi, Ariel and Ariana.

To my grandchildren present and future.

LIVE LIFE ON PURPOSE!

JW Rucker Jr.

CONTENTS

ACKNOWLEDGMENTS

To those who believe there is always more to the story.

INTRODUCTION

To the reader, this book is for encouragement and spiritual self-examination purposes only and is not intended to come from a strictly religious or scientific point of view but from inside and outside observations of our human condition. We have to keep in mind the adage, "Even a broken clock is right twice a day." I believe that we should make a diligent effort of paying attention to the spiritual principles that underline the various facets of ancient and modern religion and science within the context of daily living.

I also believe that we have to be careful not to stand in "reverential awe "of the persons who have delivered and are delivering messages to humanity from a scientific religious/philosophical point of view. We should look at those personalities as doors or gates that when walked through, provide paths to clear knowledge and understanding about ourselves and the environments that shape us as individuals. For your personal edification, I am aware of the various interpretations that perpetuate the acts of religion and science in times past and present.

Those who were entrusted with positions of leadership from the ancient to the modern world have abused and, in some cases, still abuse the privilege of having insight and knowledge of information that was and is meant for the masses. However, these so-called entrusted leaders used omission, false witness, theft, conquest, domination, and misdirection to subdue the minds of the people that have stood or are standing under their leadership whether by force or attrition.

In spite of what is occurring in the space surrounding you, at the end of the day you are left in a pocket of space pondering thoughts about yourself in the past, the near or distant future and the actions you may or may not take that concern yourself at this very moment. Therefore, without question, your next step will directly or indirectly affect or "infect" those around you. I believe that there is not a "cookie-cutter approach" to our 'personal' success.' We are not spiritually and emotionally the same. That is what makes us unique individuals if we choose to be. This book will explore the what, when, where, how, and why of "success." Notice I left out the who because of the who is YOU, the reader. Success is often viewed as external, often focusing on the material.

However, success can be qualified and quantified throughout every area of your life from watching your diabetic numbers turn normal to making the right decision to say no. These and other variables make up what I call the wholeness of success, or one can safely say the wholeness of living. I don't know your life's story or what position you are in right now, but it is my sincerest hope that you find peace and prosperity. Use this book along with many other encouraging media as a point of reference. Allow wisdom and understanding to be your guides through your life's journey as they bring you into knowledge and expand or change your personal world-view.

There is a power that is within you that is willing to reveal truths and manifest your thoughts and desires onto our physical plane of existence. I will refer to this energy as the "I AM." However, it is up to you to discover or re-discover this power. We all have experienced glimpses of it, you know those days when everything just works in your life in a miraculous series of events. These were not random events. They happened because, at some point, you aligned yourself with the universal laws and principles that govern the essence of our existence.

Many personal developers, life coaches, talk show hosts, clergy, etc. Offer their formula for a happier healthier and financially prosperous life because along with their life's journey they have met with what they would consider success in particular areas of life and would like to share it with the world.

This book will explore some of these "success formulas" and the human condition that shapes them. However, it will be up to you the reader to make an informed decision about what will work for you. Get ready to align with the power of the "I AM" in you!!

Chapter One

WHO ARE YOU?

Have you ever looked in the mirror long enough to just see you? Have you gazed into your own eyes? What were your thoughts about you? In the book "A Knock at Midnight," Dr. Martin Luther King Jr. Paraphrases Rabbi Joshua Leibman; "Before you can love other selves adequately, you've got to love your own self properly." In other words, how can you love your neighbor (which in the context of this book could be anyone; relative, friend, or foe)? If you can't first 'love' yourself? I was intrigued by two contestants on a television broadcast of a top talent competition who overcame tremendous physical, mental, and spiritual challenges to make it to the top tier of the game.

To shut out the naysayers for which I am sure there were more than a few and to quite the negative thoughts of the mind was not an easy task. How were these two contestants who have reached a level of success able to align their dreams and desires with the laws of the "I AM" and transform them from the invisible to the visible when we see so many others including ourselves struggle with simple challenges?

Earl Nightingale reminds us that "Our mind comes as standard equipment at birth. It's free and things that are given to us for nothing, we place little value on." So, some of us (humans) understand considerably the gifts that we were given and show gratitude by taking possession of them and using them rightly. What are these "gifts?" Spirit, conscious thought, body, hopes, dreams, and love. Humans are equipped with these visible and invisible tools to use at our discretion without cost or penalty. These gifts are priceless. However, there are external systems

visible and invisible that fight to control your free gifts with or without your permission. Each order that comprises our social construct is headed by what I call "gatekeepers."

Be aware of gatekeepers some could be benevolent while others can be malevolent. Gatekeepers can manifest in the form of your own conscious thought or an idea or the suggestion of another human being. Either way, they will use some type of persuasion or distraction that can alter your present view(s) therefore, possibly influencing your decision(s). For example, a young lady has her sights set on being in the music industry. She has won many local and national talent competitions, but the young singer still has not reached her goal of receiving a recording contract. Finally, the day arrives when she has the opportunity to audition for a major record producer. We find our young singer anxiously waiting in the studio lobby along with several hopefuls. Suddenly the door opens, and the producer's assistant pointed to one of the talents in waiting and gestured for her to come in. Then without warning the assistant approaches our young singer and discreetly tells her that artists like her are not in high demand right now and if she wants, she could reschedule her audition for another time.

However, the singer was determined. She paused for a moment and said to herself… *"Keep on asking, and you will receive what you ask for. Keep on seeking, and you will find. Keep on knocking, and the door will be opened to you.* Our young singer turned to the assistant with a smile and told her, 'I choose to stay and wait for my turn in line.' Her choice to stay and wait paid off. Our young singer signed a very lucrative music contract several weeks after the audition. The singer held the key to get past this particular gatekeeper. This same key can and will open gates for you and me. In the context of her life, the singer did not view or take this as a religious statement but as a law of the universe set in place by the "I AM."

Your mind is a point of attack for outside forces every day. The history of the human condition confirms this over and over again. However, it is up to you to examine the evidence presented by your real-life experiences of what you see and hear through a plethora of electronic and print mediums, as well as conversations with others. A review of Edward Bernays book "Propaganda" explains it this way. "It remains a fact that in almost every act of our daily lives.

Whether in the sphere of politics or business, in our social conduct or our ethical thinking, we are dominated by the relatively small number of persons—a trifling fraction of our hundred and twenty million—who understand the mental processes and social patterns of the masses. It is they who pull the wires which control the public mind, who harness old social forces and contrive new ways to bind and guide the world." Who or what is influencing your thoughts at this moment? Most often, we tend to let our mind wander into past and future events and barely remain in the now. The "I AM" which was, is, and which is to come to exist on all three planes, but it is the now or the "is" of the "I AM" to which we should align.

There is nothing wrong with using past experiences to navigate through a right now event or daydream about a future filled with promises and the goal(s) you desire to achieve. However, a lot of people and you may know some of them tend to dwell either in the past or are pre-occupied with tomorrow and it is the NOW that seems to get very little attention. I have locked myself out of my house, left my keys in the car, and just misplaced things in a matter of seconds. Why because I have put the now on automatic pilot and have not slowed down enough to pay attention to it. Not giving your attention to the NOW can also come with a hefty price.

Where are your thoughts today? Are they usually open and ready for a favorable opportunity or encounter? Are you really paying attention to the ideas and conversations of your colleagues and loved ones? Are you in "the NOW" or in the past or tomorrow? David J. Lieberman, in his book "You Can Read Anyone," states that "Human nature is the hardware running the program we call "thought" - input in, input out. It does the same thing every time, based upon the commands entered."

The question is, why does the "mind" do the same thing every time? The reason is that the subconscious is programmed from birth until the age of seven or so. These what I call, foundational programs are inputs from your environment. I believe it (programming) starts at the first breath taken outside of the womb. You cannot rush your authentic success, like any story, it has to have a beginning a middle and end. But this is not any story; it is your story. I believe in gaining a better understanding of yourself, you have to start at the cellular level.

According to Dr. Bruce Lipton, "You are made out of 50 trillion cells, and each cell is a living entity within itself. You are a community, not a single person. The mind is the lord over this community of cells that make up you. If you have a benevolent lord, you're good, but if you have an unkind lord, it can be bad." In other words, the community of cells become an aligned collective (become one) and follow instructions given by the mind. This pattern of "oneness" is not only seen in modern science but is a theme of our human condition. Deuteronomy chapter 6, verse 4, reinforces this principle.

The collective world view of our biology is beginning to change. It was believed by some scientist that the body is a machine controlled by genes. However, this assumption changed in and around 1925 with the introduction of science known as quantum mechanics. Quantum scientist contest that the universe is energy and that energy flows through every being in the world according to its kind. In essence, our minds can receive and transmit this energy through your body and out of your body with your brain being the central processing unit (CPU). However, if your mind is like the central processing unit then what we call the "Universe" where it is said all energy flows to, though, and from, must be the motherboard or mainboard that allocates power and allows communication with your conscious and subconscious mind by means of frequency (waves) and vibrations. Which, in turn, can mean that our subconscious mind can be programmed.

We will get back to the science about you shortly. Your authentic success also depends on you to be mentally and physically healthy. In the past, it was thought that successful people were genetically endowed with the ability to have a disease free, wealthy, and vibrant life. Even recent studies that support those early theories (mind you they are theories and not fact) about how genes determine your life, tend to be too exclusive

"A study of more than 20,000 people in the U.K., U.S., and New Zealand found those with certain genetic variations earned more money, had better careers, and got further in education. Regardless of which class they came from, their genes could help them do better in life than their parents before them." Of course, the title of the article where the above quote originated is "Being rich and successful really is in your DNA: Being dealt the right genes determine whether you get on in life."

Let me remind you again that this is based on theory and is not a fact. It definitely is not a fact about you and your goals to reach your authentic success. Unfortunately, those so-called researchers were probably given a lot of money to place a stumbling block in front of conscious thoughts. Remember, all systems have an agenda, and some systems will do anything to keep their power and to keep the masses in an unconscious state of doubt about themselves.

PERCEPTION

Understanding perception, within the context of your authentic success, is essential. 'Perception' is the awareness of the elements of environment through physical sensation. "Perception is the switch that controls your biology." It is you and how you see the world that controls your biology starting at the cellular level. This is the science of epigenetics, which theorizes that you have control over your genes. But how can that happen? It works through your mind your very thoughts can be a catalyst for healing your body or making it sick even to the point of death. This is proven through what doctors call the "Placebo Effect." According to Dr. Lipton, what you believe, creates your life on the inside and the outside.

In a U.S. News magazine issue titled "The Secret Mind," How your unconscious really shapes your decisions." "According to neuroscientist, we are conscious of only about 5 percent of our cognitive activity, so most of our decisions, actions, emotions, and behavior depends on the 95% of brain activity that goes beyond our conscious awareness. Most of our day is spent on auto-pilot, and we are thinking consciously only 1% out of the day. So how are we functioning?

As I stated earlier, The Subconscious mind has been programmed since birth. The first five to seven years of life, your brain is in a state of "Theta" a low-frequency vibration that is close to hypnosis. So, everything that you've seen or heard in your environment positive or negative during those sensitive years is in your subconscious mind.

Knowing this is not an excuse to forfeit your authentic success. Your subconscious mind is tricky to navigate. You may say it's the devil; however, it is not some outside red dude with a tail and a pitchfork it's you. Take a deep breath. In the words of Dr. Frederick Eikerenkoetter, "It is your responsibility to define yourself; to define yourself in terms of the good that you want to be done and to have." At the beginning of this chapter, I asked the question, what do you think about you? What do you want to be? Now let me ask you with all due respect, are you living off of what someone said you are? Our societal systems attempt to program the subconscious of those who are ignorant of the power that lies within them. Terms like poor, underprivileged, inner-city, underserved, worm, sinner, may have been programmed in your subconscious mind and you allow guilt and shame to make you believe that you cannot go beyond these systems. I am sincerely asking, do not let these lies infiltrate your mind any longer.

Whatever you subconsciously define yourself as you will become that. "I am always becoming that which I am Conscious of being" It's just not enough being white black, American, etc. You are more than those surface definitions about you. "The poor remain poor because they continue to accept or define themselves as poor people." They allowed someone else to define them. Jesus said *the poor will always be with you (Matthew chapter 26 verse 11)* because you have those who will continue to think poorly about themselves, and they are what they believe themselves to be." They have learned to stick with the status quo. But I am sure that is not who you are. You have examined yourself and now understand and know that there has to be something more about you.

Hold on tight, here it is, you are "I AM" You are one with this energy. However, there are social systems that will try to create enough doubt in you so you can stay on the lemming train. You have to consciously know who you are. Whether you believe in the existence of the personalities that we read about in the books that make up what we call a Bible, Torah, Quran, Tripitaka, etc. The universal principles of life and the laws that govern them were expressed by writers who shared stories about people just like us. The personalities of Yeshua, Muhammad, and Gautama Buddha expressed a raised consciousness so that their students could see the human condition from a physical, social, philosophical, and psychological perspective and learn from it to reach a higher level of existence. However, looking at the current human condition, we can conclude that only some genuinely understand it.

The teacher from Nazareth says this. *"But small is the gate and narrow the way that leads to life, and only a few find it."* Let's take it back a little. Remember, science has found that we are conscious of only 5% of our cognitive activity, and the other 95% goes beyond our conscious awareness. Here is another coincidental kicker, according to our modern science, the self-conscious (creative mind) that generates free will circulates information at around 40 Bits per second. While the subconscious (habitual) circulates or can process in 40 million bits of data per second. These research-based findings reveal that the road to conscious thought is narrow indeed. The scientific information stated above is for your own personal edification. I suggest that you research and confirm the data for yourself to find out how it relates to you, your identity, and your authentic success.

Chapter Two

YOUR PATH

Without the power of the " I AM" human thought is bound to its primal state of... "killed or be killed," competition, and "I'll get them before they get me," These thoughts belong to the minds of primal human beings chained to a constant state of fear and anxiety. Unfortunately, we see this behavior coming from the so-called rich and powerful, everyday working class and even stay at home moms. For which the results of their behavior almost always tragically end with a physical or spiritual loss of life along with an adverse/ripple effect on many people. This statement is not by any means, downplaying those who are suffering from psychological disorders as a result of chemical imbalances, physical trauma, and medication side-effects.

However, there are those who choose to follow the path of "self" that can lead to a twisted view of the world around them. If you are on this path, there is help if you desire it. Here is an age-old example of one who rejected the power of the "I AM."

"Why are you so angry? The Lord asked Cain." Why do you look so sad? You will be accepted if you do what is right. But if you refuse to do what is right, then watch out! Sin is crouching at the door eager to control you, but you must subdue it and be its master." (Genesis 4-7 NIV).

Most of us have heard this story over and over again. However, I am asking you to step out of the realm of religion and analyze this sequence of events in its full context as it is presented in chapter four in the book of beginnings better known as Genesis.

Cain chose a path that entertained his own thoughts of fear, jealousy, and anxiety, but why? David J. Lieberman writes, "Emotional states are either self-induced, externally caused, or a combination of the two. Some of the more powerful ones include guilt, fear, intimidation, appeal to ego, curiosity, and the desire to be liked and loved. When operating in any of these states, your judgment is likely to be impaired." In the case of Cain, it ended in murder. In his book "Everyman a King," Orison Sweet Marden writes, "If you are selfish, you cannot help radiating the selfish thought. Everybody about you will feel your meanness and will measure you accordingly." Now you may say I am not selfish, at least I do not think I am. To figure this out, you will have to step outside of yourself.

Two good measures are... Do you enjoy creating "win, win" situations for you and others? Do you have compassion for others without asking "what's in it for me"? Self is formally defined as "a person's essential being that distinguishes them from others, especially considered as the object of introspection or reflective action." I believe that it would be safe to say that "self" is the sum of your thoughts, which is the essence of your creative being. You were created from a spirit, a power greater than yourself. This power the "I AM" invites you (a product of creation) alongside it's being to become a direct conduit of creativity within the world you were born into. Yes, you were born to create.

You're very being (heart, mind, and soul) is like fertile soil. Seeds of thought or suggestion will always blow into your ears. Once heard, your conscious and subconscious will be ready for you the master of your ideas to help geminate or terminate potential influences. Scott Shickler and Jeff Walker in their book "The 7 Mindsets," explain the results of scientific research as it relates to your thoughts. " It's estimated that approximately 65,000 thoughts go through our minds every day. About ninety-five percent, these thoughts are the exact thoughts we had the day before and the day before that. What's on our minds basically stays. This wouldn't be so bad, except about eighty percent of our thoughts are fueled by negativity."

Friend, I don't know what path you are on right now, but I do know that your life's path is constructed by your thoughts. Every thought creates and drives your next "right now" step regardless of your present circumstance. Before you make that next step, consider your current thinking remember whether those thoughts are positive or negative, if you allow them to grow you are accountable for the harvest because you were trusted with the power to create them. To align with the power of the "I AM," you must take accountability for past incidents and negative feelings, those doors bust be closed. You can start by forgiving yourself. I have learned that we, as humans, have no right to demean ourselves mentally or physically and continue to beat our-self's up because of what we believe were mistakes that we can't recover from. You might ask why I don't have the right to do that.

Although you are a creative being and the master of your thoughts, you did not create yourself. I would like to introduce you to a man whose past was filled with misdeeds and self-doubt, and then one day, the proverbial light bulb came on, and he finally realized his purpose and realigned himself with the " I AM" this was his AH-HA moment. *"I praise you because I am fearfully and wonderfully made; your works are wonderful; I know that full well." (Psalm139: 14)* Read and understand the story of King David and his relationship with the "I AM" in its full context, and you will see that he (David) was no better a human than you are. However, David and earthly king understood the laws set in place by a power greater than himself.

I challenge you to take note of David's statement and use this as a daily positive affirmation and allow it to germinate within your thoughts as you create your next "right now step." Don't get it twisted, remember the law of sowing and reaping. Whatever seeds you have sown they will manifest in some form or another but do not be discouraged and feed on the negative *"Go and sin no more" read* John 8:9-11 in context to receive a better understanding of this declaration. Do not allow anyone to judge you and hold you to guilt and shame. Remember you are free! Exercise your new freedom by loving the "I AM" with all of your heart, mind, and soul and love others as you love yourself because all of the law and the words of the ancient prophets are based on these two declarations.

Well, you might think about why I would want to do that? I do not understand the "Bible" or why should I love others? The "I AM" is within you so if you can't love yourself, you cannot 'love' the "I AM" therefore you cannot 'love' your neighbor as yourself. Take a deep breath and let that soak in. The bible is not a religious book. In entirety, the "bible" is a compilation of ancient but relevant writings that describe the human condition and the laws that were established by the "I AM" that in-turn we can align with to live an abundant life. We were not created without instructions.

However, in the time of the emperor Constantine politics clouded the original message. In his book " Fabricating Faith: How Christianity Became a Religion Jesus would Have Rejected" Richard Hagenston writes "There was a time when traditional Christian doctrine need not have become what it is today, but early church leaders made the choices that they felt would most benefit them. As a result, in a kind of religious Darwinism, Christianity evolved more to fulfill an agenda of creating converts to enhance the status and fortunes of the church than to respect the teachings of the man for whom it was named."

Now about loving others. There is a cultural experience called "emotional contagion" like passing germs we can pass our moods. In a 2018 Time Magazine article, Alexandra Sifferlin writes, "A 2008 study reported that when a nearby friend is happy, happiness can spread among that person's social group and even increase your own happiness up to 25%." Professor Sigal Barsade and her research colleagues found that people who are employed in a culture of "companionate love-affection, caring and compassion" were more satisfied with their jobs and retained consistent job attendance. With this small glimpse of the effects of loving others, I challenge you to test this law set in place by the "I AM" for yourself.

As stated before, we are surrounded by and influenced by systems. When we understand how they operate, we can keep a closer watch on our hearts and minds. The psychological ploy of scarcity is often used by compliance experts to "trick" people into falling in-line. In the context of employment, we will receive messages through the media that competition is stiff for "high paying jobs," and people are lined up to get an opportunity. However, this ploy pushes many to settle for a lesser vocation and eventually pushes you further and further to become a cog in the wheel of this worlds seemingly finite matrix. Sadly, most people believe this is what you have to do. If you follow the laws set forth by the "I AM," you will soon realize that competition as it relates to the workplace is just an illusion.

Earl Nightingale stated this some decades ago. "That's why today, there isn't really any competition unless we make it for ourselves. instead of competing for all we have to do is to create." Another system that can cause moral dilemmas that can compromise our right alignment (righteousness) with the "I AM" is what I consider a sub-system of a few other systems, including the legal system. However, we will get to that shortly. Remember the "I AM" is in you and knows your heart and mind better than you do. The ancient prophet Jeremiah was reminded of this. "The heart is deceitful above all things and beyond cure who can understand it? I the Lord search the heart and examine the mind, to reward a man according to his conduct, according to what his deeds deserve." (Jeremiah 17:9-10).

With that said, Deborah Tannen author of "The Argument Culture: Stopping America's War of Words," shares her views about the "adversarial system." "You have been told many times if you're in a traffic accident, "never admit fault." This is one of the costs of the adversary system and perhaps one of the most damaging ones: It disrupts human impulses toward honesty and corrupts human relationships. This is hurtful to the human spirit." This brings us to the age-old battle of good versus evil, and as you can conclude, this battle begins in your thoughts. All I will say about this is there are existing invisible systems and people that intend to deceive, distract, demoralize and provide a false sense of security; especially when the positive thoughts that you are cultivating towards a successful goal are made known.

In late November of 2017, I had an opportunity to visit Lakewood Church in Houston, Texas. Pastor Joel Osteen's sermon title was "Pit Praisers," and he began to expound on the well-known Bible story of Joseph. Joseph believed he was going places. However, his life was not without distraction and disappointment. For which, I truly believe his journey really began in that cistern. His brothers plotted to kill him; all save one (Judah or Reuben) who had a "compassionate" thought and devised a plan to save his brother. What was going through Joseph's (whose name in Hebrew means "Increase") mind while he was down in that cistern? Could you imagine, he had evil gatekeepers in the form of his brothers above him and the gatekeepers of his own thoughts swirling through in his mind. Somehow, as you read his story in context, it would lead one to conclude that Joseph never lost focus of his dreams from beginning to end and believed he was the righteous (in-right alignment) man that the "I AM" created him to be. Joseph fulfilled his life's purpose through active, meaningful, and "right now" decision. You can read the story of Joseph in the book of Beginnings (Genesis) Chapter 37 and the Qur'an Chapter 12. Please do not look at this from a religious point of view but a view of our human condition.

Chapter Three

CIRCUMSTANCE

The 19th Century Victorian writer James Allen 1864-1912 wrote an essay entitled "As a Man Thinketh." In that essay, Allen writes about the "Effect of Thought on Circumstances" Now, If you understood the story of Joseph from a human point of view, it is our circumstances, some that we create for our-self and some not of our making and your thoughtful response to them that can either make you or break you.

Allen says, "Man is buffeted by circumstances so long as he believes himself to be the creature of external conditions, but when he realizes that he is a creative power and that he may command the hidden soil and seeds of his being out of which circumstances grow. He then becomes the rightful master of himself." We learned this earlier with the story of Cain. One can remain in the proverbial "pit" and brood over filthy and hurtful thoughts of what others have done and are doing to you and what you have done to yourself and never bare the excellent fruit the "I AM" has created you to bring forth. To reinforce this the "I AM" declares; He knows the plans he has for you. "to prosper you and not to harm you, plans to give you hope and a future" (Jeremiah 29:11).

Proverbial wisdom tells us that, rich or poor, we were all created by the power of the "I AM." A person who considers his or herself materially wealthy could very well be in a circumstance where he or she is void of right-thinking and face the real possibilities of spiritual and physical bankruptcy. Could this be you right now? If so, arrest and terminate your negative thoughts immediately because prison or sadly, mental or physical death is waiting.

As a student of the human condition, I have seen those with good ideas for gaining material wealth become "successful." However, the subtle whispers of greed, gluttony, and deception infiltrated and were germinated to create a circumstance (a pit if you will) that defiles the laws of the "I AM" and negatively impacts others. An example of this would be the so-called investment gurus and their actions before and during the "great recession" of 2007.

There were and probably still are individuals who promise unreasonable returns for modest investments. There are so many testimonies presented in a wide range of mediums from television to seminars of people who trusted a family member, friend, or brokerage firm that seemingly had it all together, with their money to find out later that they were deceived. Now the person who initiated the fraud begins to play a game of financial whack a mole to keep up a fraudulent reputation while the ones who were deceived try to figure out how did this happen to them. If this is you, take accountability for your thoughts and do not place blame on the circumstance.

Arrest your negative thoughts and terminate them. Give thanks and praise to the "I AM" within you believing that you, a creative being was created by a power higher than you and your circumstance. Keep your thoughts away from the concerns of past and future. It is your next **Right-Now** move that will have the most significant impact. Now take a deep breath. Remember, your journey to overcome your circumstance starts with trusting the "I AM."

"I have observed something else under the sun. The fastest runner doesn't always win the race, and the strongest warrior doesn't always win the battle. The wise sometimes go hungry, and the skillful are not necessarily wealthy. And those who are educated don't always lead successful lives. It is all decided by chance, by being in the right place at the right time." Eccl 9:11 NLT.

You may read this part of scripture and say Ah Ha I knew it was all chance and sarcastically say why do I even try. However, further research into this passage will give you a clear picture of what the passage actually means. The fast, reliable, wise, and educated are observed being in these positions because they depend on their own strength to succeed. They (the people in these positions) never consider the consequences of their right now thoughts and the timing of their next move. All of these things should prudently be found. In the Hebrew translation, chance in this context can be seen as time or opportunity and being in the right place translates to an incident or Occurrence. These things are part of the human condition for those who do not trust the power of the I AM.

Bible commentator Adam Clark says that… "Every man has what may be called time and space to act in, an opportunity to do a particular work. But in this Time and Opportunity there is *Incident*, what may fall in; and *Occurrence*, what may meet and frustrate an attempt. These things should be wisely weighed, and seriously balanced; for those four things belong to every human action. While you have *time*, seek an *Opportunity* to do what is right; but calculate on hinderances and oppositions, because time and opportunity have their Incident and Occurrence."

James Allen reminds us that "Suffering is always the effect of wrong thought in some direction. It is an indication that the individual is out of harmony with himself, with the law of his being." If you choose to acknowledge, understand and align with the invisible laws of sowing and reaping, repentance (changing your mindset), giving and receiving, asking, loving the "I AM" with the essence of your being, loving others and loving yourself a Kingdom has genuinely come to you.

This is not a religious statement. The messenger Yahushua (Jesus) whether you think of Him as a Prophet, Messiah, Lord, or Great Teacher. He presented and still presents himself as a door that is to be opened to a new way of life here on earth. A system above systems if you will, that offers true freedom, not a religion.

Religion misunderstands this concept and continues to cloud our thoughts by continuously worshiping the door instead of opening it and walking into a better way of living. "Law, not confusion is the dominating principle in the universe; Justice, not injustice is the soul and substance of life; and righteousness, not corruption, is the molding and moving force in the spiritual government of the world. This being so, man has but search himself to find the universe is right, and during the process of putting himself right, he will find that as he alters his thoughts toward things and other people, things and other people will alter towards him" (James Allen).

Friend, your success cannot be generalized, you have to be patient. I know it is tough to say and easy to do because you may feel that you have to act now. We all know tomorrow is not promised to us, but it is by faith whether you believe it or not that we look towards tomorrow, so be patient and live! This is one thing I know about success; it is authentic to you and only you. Your values, world view, proclivities, and your moral compass is attached to your success, and all of these are driven by your thoughts. Understanding the "subsystems" of authority, compliance, and obedience can help you thoughtfully defend or entirely free you from adverse circumstances that may contain these subsystems.

There are many groups and organizations that people belong to and/or associated with. From religious institutions to senior citizens groups, there's a plethora of organizations (systems) that many people are members of and submit to more than one. Our creative and right now thoughts can be influenced by these organizations. The desire to belong is human nature. We may wear paraphernalia, paste our cars with bumper stickers, fly flags, and give money for what we believe to be a "good cause."

Members in groups become authentic sources of persuasion. Dan Crosby writes, "Our need to relate to our in-groups often guides our behavior and decision-making, a trait that can be used against us by compliance professionals." Needless to say, compliance professionals are not your only concern. In the 1960s, Psychology professor Stanley Milgram performed experiments that included these three subsystems and how humans behave under what I call perceived authority, which can also mimic 'real authority.' I believe it is worth examining Milgram's experiments to gain an in-depth understanding of this well-documented view of the human condition. Some may call it brainwashing, conditioning, or just plain old charisma. However, it is a psychological wonder how humans give way to other humans who are seen as "authority" figures. Your Right Now, thoughts can be easily clouded by a person accent, weight, skin color, clothing, vehicle, home, etc. Why do people who were created to create and become the masters of their own thoughts fall victim to abuse from those who have so-called authority?

Milgram's experiment that was conducted in the context of compliance and administration revealed that if a person (subject) were told by a so-called authority figure (a guy in a lab coat) to knowingly hurt a colleague, in this case, another participant. She or he would obey that authority figure without thought. However, when the role of the authority figure was given to another participant, his or her directives were questioned because of their appearance and the presumption of their lack of degreed knowledge. Circumstances and change can drive an individual to unknowingly turn over his or her gift of creative authority, could it happen to you? Dr. Robert B. Cialdini, the author of "Influence: The Psychology of Persuasion," came to this conclusion as it relates to Milgram's findings. "There are sobering implications of this finding for those concerned about the ability of another form of authority-government to extract freighting levels of obedience from ordinary citizens."

I wonder if Dr. Cialdini and Milgram had a crystal ball and saw the 2016 presidential election along with its baggage of allegations including another country influencing said election by psychologically influencing American voters through social media and other electronic forms of mass communication. If the claims lend anything to the truth, how many individuals, who are blessed with the gift to master their own thoughts unwittingly surrender those thoughts to a malevolent gatekeeper of an invisible subsystem? So how can I avoid circumstances that involve mass deception? Verifying the source. Sometimes we tend to act or react too quickly to an "authentic source" giving up our gift of creative thought because we lend our minds to the credibility of the person or system that is put before us. Take a moment or a few days to get a clear picture of the motivation of the system or person who desires your buy-in and conformity. Are they trying to get to know you better, isolate you from family or friends, attack your self-esteem, and use us versus them agenda?

This also applies to those systems or persons you plan on making a purchase from, asking expert advice, making a financial investment, or giving personal and confidential information. To combat this be conscious and purposeful about your 'right now thought's in other words, as my mother would say pray about it and seek wise counsel. I wish I would have followed her advice before I purchased my time-share.

Be aware that the person(s) providing the information have trained themselves either formally or informally to become an expert or to be perceived as an expert about the subject or system where his/her persuasion can be targeted. For example, a person who is known to have been in education for several years could be asked by a family member or friend what is the best way for their son or daughter to organize a homework binder.

The person who asked the educator the question considers the educator as one who would help their child solve a problem. No matter the method the educator advises the student to use in organizing a binder, the parent who asked the question will accept it as truth because the educator is purportedly known to be a reliable source. I hope you understand that part of your sustained success depends on your ability to discern what works for you. I will end this chapter with words from wisdom herself.

I call to you to all of you! I raise my voice to all people. You simple people, use good judgment. You foolish people, show some understanding. Listen to me! I have important things to tell you. Everything I say is right, for I speak the truth and detest every kind of deception.

Proverbs 8:4-7 NLT

Chapter Four

A GOOD NAME

H ave you ever met a successful recluse? There may be a few who have inherited wealth. I am talking about a person who has gained what I call authentic success that worked from the ground floor. Your 'authentic success' cannot and will not be created in isolation. I said you will not be because your attitude, swag, charisma or whatever you choose to call it impacts everyone you come in contact with. Orison Sweett Marden in his book Every Man A King writes "Success is not dependent solely on our earnest affirmation, on our self-confidence, but also on the confidence of others in us; but this confidence is very largely a reflection of our own, the effect of our own personality on them."

Do you believe that you can have an effect on the moods of others? When you walk into your office, classroom, locker room, etc. What are your predictions about your day? You may say just let me get through this, or you may really have the thought of putting in a breakout effort just to show your bosses and colleagues that you can get the job done. Either way, suggestions made by your body language and the presentation of your thoughts are being watched by those around you and believe me, those people will react to you accordingly.

Whether your future plans are to become CEO of your own company, introduce a life-changing invention, become the next breakout superstar, or just be a better bathroom attendant, your success will depend on your "good name." This is not a call to action for you to become a people pleaser. There are many who the public perceives as successful because of his or her global, national, or local celebrity. However, we often see some of these "successful" individuals tied up in scandal and innuendo because of unseen proclivities. The unusual flip-side of this is that the public sometimes rewards them for allowing their inclinations to be seen in a light that is a false positive. So, with that twisted view, their celebrity or brand inflates like a balloon waiting to burst and burst it will.

With that said, is success fleeting? Some may say yes. However, I believe what I call authentic success is not. Many have achieved this success by believing in the power of the "I Am." The "I Am" is the cornerstone on which 'authentic success' is made. If you decide to build upon this cornerstone, it will not look perfect all of the time. Sometimes it will look downright ugly, especially when you're trying to establish your right name. A "good name" can be ruined before anyone gets to know it because of an inconsistency in the way one thinks. This cannot align with the power of the I AM. Self-doubt and mean words from nay-sayers can cloud your judgment and affect your right now thoughts so the confidence that you aspire to project from within may not be seen. Marden puts it this way. "Why should we drag our weaknesses through life when a little common sense, a little right thinking in fixing new habits of thought would soon remedy them?"

Persistence and kindness are elements of securing a "good name" and the favor of the "I AM" and others around you. There is a good story among many that illustrate this. You will find it in the book of Ruth, chapter 2 verses, 11-13. As I asked before, do not look at this from a religious perspective. This story read in context shows authentic success as a beautiful part of the human condition. These same principles for having a "good name" can help you because they still apply today. In his book "The Wealth Choice," author Dennis Kimbrough interviews Radio executive Kathy Hughes. In her story, a "good name" and faith in the "I AM" granted her favor along the journey to authentic success. Mrs. Hughes describes one of her favorable encounters. "Looking back, I made 32 presentations, and I was denied each time. Ironically, I gave my thirty-third presentation to a female banker in New York. Before I could finish my pitch, we shook hands on a deal. Chemical bank loaned me $ 600,000 and gave me the push I needed."

Wisdom makes this statement in the book of Proverbs about loyalty and kindness. She (wisdom) puts an exclamation point on these two virtues because if you continue in them, you will find favor with God and people, and you will earn a good reputation. Or as the English Standard Version reads; "So you will find favor and good success in the sight of God and man." Your passion can be contagious and draw others closer to you, and you closer to authentic success. It's not a matter of why you spend hours each day doing what you do. It is the manner in how you do it.

People may not immediately remember your name. However, your actions will surely leave a lasting impression. The reality shows Undercover Boss and Shark Tank are examples of this part of the human condition. Darren Hardy Author of The Entrepreneur Roller Coaster writes about his former housekeeper Leticia who showed a passion for how she got her job done. "And as for Leticia? Sadly, she is no longer working for us. We lost her to someone with a massive estate who tripled her salary-and made her the estate manager. That's what happens when you flip the switch of your passion ON. Opportunity finds you, and people beat a path to your door."

When you hear a familiar name, whether famous or not, what are your thoughts about that person? Do you see that person in a positive or negative light based solely on his or her name? It's ok to say yes because it happens as a part of our human condition. However, we have to be careful not to pass judgment (present negative emotions) on a person because of their name. Well, you might say that just doesn't happen in our modern society; names are not that important when it comes to success.

Further reading of this chapter may change your current view about your name and success or lend credence to things you already knew. Remember Leticia, the housekeeper I mentioned earlier? Well, that name is rooted in the Latin word Laetitia, which means joy, gladness, and delight. New York University professor Adam Alter believes that to an extent names seem to dictate one's fortune. There is a word for it, and it is called Nominative

Determinism. "It's possible that you are drawn to what your name keeps reminding you about." For example, the famed plumber Thomas Crapper. Although he did not invent the toilet, he became successful in building a plumbing company that held positive notoriety because of the quality of its products.

New York Businessman Michael Ayer and his wife named their son Billion. Sixteen years later Billion says that "Being named Billion Ayer, you stand out more and people I've never met know me. But I don't even know their name."

In Billions case and many others like him, they possess a built-in reputation that can lead them to great authentic success if they should choose to follow the path. Nevertheless, your last name does not have to be Keys to play a piano or Bolt to win gold medals, and if your first name is Joe, it does not make you average if you don't want to be. Your name, whatever it is, can be a powerful tool that can lead to your authentic success. Having a name and identity is a hidden rule in cultures around the world. "This bestowal of name and identity is a kind of symbolic contract between society and the individual. Seen from one side of the contract, by giving a name the society confirms the individual's existence and acknowledges its responsibilities toward that person."

The name Moses (Moshe in Hebrew) means to pull or draw out of water. It was appropriate for the daughter of an Egyptian Pharaoh to give him that name because that is where this infant was found. However, I believe she did not realize that her adopted son will draw out his people from Egypt. One might say this is a coincidence, divine provocation, or use our new modern term "Nominative Determinism." The part of this story that reflects our human condition is that Moses felt unworthy of the task to lead the people of Israel out of Egypt. Moses's name was already recognized by the people as an Egyptian Prince, not as the leader of Israel's emancipation.

In verses thirteen and fourteen in the book of Exodus, it reads. But Moses protested, *"If I go to the people of Israel and tell them, 'The God of your ancestors has sent me to you,' they will ask me,*

'What is his name?' Then what should I tell them?" The Lord
replied to Moses, "I Am Who I Am. Say this to the people of Israel:
I Am has sent me to you." I believe the tribes of Jacob (Israel)
needed a definitive answer as to which God sent Moses to them.
Why? Because the Egyptian culture recognized many gods and
those so-called gods had names like Rah, Isis, etc. Unlike the titles
El, Elohim, El Shaddai, and Jehovah; it "I Am" is a definitive
name.

According to Matthew Henry's commentary, four attributes set
the "I Am" apart from the other titles. The first is that it is self-
existent. Second, it is eternal, always the same. Third, it checks all
inquiries concerning the name of God. Fourth, the name is faithful
and immutable. "What was done at this time, by the authority of
God himself, was to select from among the epithets one to be
distinctly a proper name, and at the same time explain its true
meaning as something more than "The Existent" as really "The
Alone Existent" the source of all existence."

So how does your name factor into your authentic success?
What do you think people will say when your name is mentioned
in casual conversation? Will your name cause people to rally
behind your business or career? Remember, in building your
success, you need people. Hopefully, it will be people that foster
and encourage positive motivations. Does your work ethic give
you a name that people trust?

Do you feel worthy of pursuing and managing success no
matter how it comes? Aligning with the "I Am" that is within you
will give you the ability to carefully manage your right now
thoughts and allow you to boldly believe that you are authentically
successful because you are backed by and aligned with a
guaranteed name. That name can make your name shine like a light
on a hill. The other side of this is yes you can run on your own
steam believing your name or brand is a product of your hard work
resulting in material success. However, if you had to lie cheat steal
or even kill (metaphorically speaking) to obtain it, how long do
you expect your "good name" and "success" to last?

Friend, of course, you may not agree with the words written

here and how they relate to success. Remember not to look at this from a religious point of view but a view of our human condition that transcends time itself. Your authentic success depends on you the whole you. Not some random outside thought or idea that someone has about you. For a lot of us, our name is where our journey to authentic success starts whether big or small. You may have changed your original name to something that will draw more attention to you, or you did it to get rid of the past. Regardless of your right now situation, your good name and the character behind it is a valuable possession that can be secured (if you choose) by the "I Am" that lives within you.

Chapter Five

NOT YOUR WORRY

I t is ok to be compassionate. As a matter of fact, compassion is an integral part of the human race. You and I were created to love, show compassion, empathize, be angry, regretful, etc. However, worry, which I believe is the polar opposite of concern and can cause mental, spiritual, and physical decline can stifle your 'Authentic Success.' I think we worry too much about others, situations beyond our mortal control, and the thoughts of others about us. Throughout history, the human condition as it is related to worry has not changed. Dale Carnegie wrote, "Our fatigue is often caused not by work, but by worry, frustration, and resentment." Singer Demi Lovato says, "I try to keep it real. I don't have time to worry about what I'm projecting to the world. I'm just busy being myself."

"Therefore, do not worry about tomorrow, for tomorrow will worry about itself. Each day has enough trouble of its own"

Matthew 6:34(NIV)

Remember, this is not a religious statement. It should be a part of the 'I AM' that is within you. Researchers at the University of Surrey reported worry as "chain of thoughts and images that are effectively negative and relatively uncontrollable." We can conclude from this statement, the writings of Matthew and other quotes related to worry that worry has been a part of the human condition since the 'fall of man' (read the book of beginnings a.k.a Genesis chapter 3). Fear can lead to anxiety, which, in my opinion, is a(n) enemy of the mind. There are even pharmaceuticals legal and otherwise that are created to keep this demon at bay. According to Amanda Chan, "Research has shown that anxiety can take a toll on sleep, tax your immune system, raise your risk of post-traumatic stress disorder, and even affect your risk of dying from a disease." Anxiety can definitely derail your 'authentic success.

"Worry is the interest paid by those who borrow trouble."

- George Washington

Worrying about others and/or taking on their problems can put a strain on you and slow your journey to 'authentic success.' Worrying about things we can't control, for example, the thoughts and feelings of others can cause us to create scenarios that are not real. "We thrive when we get along with others and think and act independently at the same time. If you aren't doing both, you're out of balance, and your psyche will complain about it with either depression ("No one likes me.") or anxiety ("I have to get them to like me"). These are often warning signs, and if not heeded, things can get terrible. That's why it's dangerous to worry too much what others think about you."

Right now, you are on your way to the point of success, whether it's to pay off all of your credit cards or start a new business. Your overall 'authentic success' is made up of small achievements, much like atoms that make up matter. All of this will involve other people, along with their opinions, critiques, and encouragements. So how can you avoid the pitfalls of worrying about people and situations beyond your control?

I am not looking at this through rose-colored glasses. We as humans can't stop caring what everyone thinks. However, we can surround ourselves with positive people who have our best interest at heart, therefore, narrowing the opportunity for negative people to come into our space. These positive people, family, friends, or your community will sow seeds of love into your life.

...But correct the wise, and they will love you. Instruct the wise, and they will be even wiser.

Teach the right-minded, and they will learn even more.

- Proverbs 9:8-9

What can you do when someone thinks wrongly of you? I would suggest that you "brush it off" because when we are trying to please everyone, we are not being true to ourselves. In your current occupation, or in your future business where you are the boss, some people will dislike you because of the shoes you wear. Take a deep breath and let it go because you are on the way to something big, and it will be bigger than yourself.

Journaling, reading scriptures, using psychotherapy, and finding your happy spot can keep you on course to your 'Authentic Success.' Gary Trosclair writes, "To remember or learn what you want, need and believe you'll need to have periods when you can hear yourself without worrying about the voices of others." In previous chapters, I talk about your' right now thoughts' and how they can help you move away from future or past beliefs. However, there is a plethora of literature that concentrates on "Hypothetical Thoughts" or what we often call "what ifs."

Our minds can make up scenarios based on partial truths either seen or heard, and those thoughts can wreck careers, relationships, and possibly, derail your pursuits of success. As I write this book, the current structure of our diverse society is fractured. Politics is casting a spell on the human psyche, particularly in the U.S. where we are not seeing each other as people anymore. Lack of compassion and patience for others has some in our society looking upon others as evil enemies because of their ethnicity, social and cultural beliefs, sexual preference, and party affiliation. I believe that creativity, (which is a character trait of the I AM that is within all of us) is being overpowered by selfishness and fear.

"What's in it for me?" and "What about me?" are questions that some may ask themselves when they are in a primal state of mind. However, there are those in our society whether they have a little or a lot that will give they're all for positive growth towards our human condition. How will all of these issues impact my 'authentic success'?

These things bring on unwanted worry if those issues continue to be at the forefront of our everyday conversations and thoughts. Authentic success for you could mean overcoming an illness. From my own experience, allowing your disease to overtake your thoughts and conversations can and in most cases, will make it worse. The enemy of the mind will use your worry/anxiety to trigger the emotion of impatience.

Once a person becomes impatient, she or he will forget about the power of the IAM that lives inside of them and turn to their own understanding. Once our illness is discovered, we start to rush the healing process instead of understanding that in most cases, it is going to take time, patience, and wisdom. I am very much aware that this is a sensitive subject for a lot of us. So, I will leave you with this example.

If a person who does not feel well ignores even the simple cough because she or he is in pursuit of achieving their goals (promotion, fame, etc.) that simple cough can eventually stop you prematurely if it is not taken care of. I also understand 'job pressures' can cause one to worry. People on your job, whether supervisor or co-worker cannot take priority over your life. In Matthew 6:25-34, Jesus shares why we should not worry:

"Therefore, I tell you, do not worry about your life, what you will eat or drink; or about your body, what you will wear. Is not life more than food, and the body more than clothes? Look at the birds of the air; they do not sow or reap or store away in barns, and yet your heavenly Father feeds them. Are you not much more valuable than they? Can anyone of you by worrying add a single hour to your life?

"And why do you worry about clothes? See how the flowers of the field grow. They do not labor or spin. Yet I tell you that not even Solomon in all his splendor was dressed like one of these. If that is how God clothes the grass of the field, which is here today and tomorrow is thrown into the fire, will he not much more clothe you-you of little faith? So do not worry, saying, 'What shall we eat?' or 'What shall we drink?' or 'What shall we wear?' For the pagans run, after all these things, and your heavenly Father knows that you need them. But seek first his kingdom and his righteousness, and all these things will be given to you as well. Therefore, do not worry about

tomorrow, for tomorrow will worry about itself. Each day has enough trouble of its own."

Chapter Six

HOW FAR WILL YOU GO?

I often speak about viewing the Bible form a perspective of our human condition and not as a religious book. Recent and past history allows us to take a look into the lives of those who came before us. Of course, some of human history has become legend and myth and is romanticized by the vivid imaginations of those in the film and publishing industry. Also, there are systems put in place to purposely blur the lines between historical fact and fiction. I believe this is done to control the minds and hearts of our various ethnicities.

However, there is one thing that sticks out about our human history that transcends those, as mentioned above. I believe it is the innate human ability to preserve for a cause. History tells us about one man who never identified himself as a god but presented his relationship with the 'I AM' as One. This man, known in his culture as Yeshua who we now call Jesus was by all purpose's human and divine. However, it is his role within the human condition that will be our focus for now. Here we Go!! From the book of Luke, chapter 19, verses 33-38: *As they were untying the colt, its owners asked them, "Why are you untying the colt?" They (His Disciples) brought it to Jesus, they threw their cloaks on the colt and put Jesus on it. As he went along, people spread their cloaks on the road. When he came near the place where the road goes down to the Mount Of Olives, the whole crowd of disciples began joyfully to praise God in loud voices for all the miracles they had seen; "Blessed is the king who comes in the name of the Lord" "Peace in heaven and glory in the Highest!"*

Now we can see the people singing and shouting their praises to the "I AM" for sending a savior who would deliver them from a system of mental spiritual and physical oppression. In the context of our human condition, we (humans) are always looking for "The one" whether it is in the realm of sports, music, film, and politics we find ourselves often talking about who is the "G.O.A.T. (greatest of all time). We sing their praises, welcome them into venues and establishments with open arms, and give them the keys to the city both literally and figuratively. If a person who was once announced as great and previously treated like royalty happens to fall victim or prey to a "system" praises turn to ridicule doubtful words, long stares, hurtful whispers begin to circulate, then all material endorsements and privileges are revoked either delaying or aborting their journey towards their cause. Now, do not get it twisted, there are those who intend to go as far as hurting and deceiving others for their authentic success. But we are not talking about them right now.

We are focusing on those who are in right alignment with the I AM those whose missions and intentions help to positively shape the world we live in. Jesus warned his disciples about the ugliness of the human condition. And how their common goal to spread the good news of the I AM's kingdom will be hindered by those who don't understand its message and by those who do understand but choose to embrace and protect societies status quo. Luke 21:12-19 reflects this. It reads …

"But before all this, they will seize you and persecute you. They will hand you over to synagogues and put you in prison, and you will be brought before kings and governors, and all on account of my name. And so you will bear testimony to me. But make up your mind not to worry beforehand how you will defend yourselves. I will give you words and wisdom that none of your adversaries will be able to resist or contradict. You will be betrayed even by parents, brothers and sisters, relatives, and friends, and they will put some of you to death. Everyone will hate you because of me. But not a hair of your head will perish. Stand firm, and you will win life.

Let's look at this passage from the human condition. On your journey towards your authentic success, you have to keep the end in mind. in verse 19 of the passage, as mentioned earlier, Jesus said, "Stand firm, and you will win life." We must first have to believe that our goals will be achieved. We are given a choice to make up our minds that we will not worry about the distractions that come along the way. We have to understand that everyone will not see your vision, even those in your own family and will try to interrupt your course.

Although Jesus speaks about physical death in verse 16, I believe that in the context of this writing, we can safely say that some people will try to murder your success mentally and spiritually. Once they have killed the spirit of your goal with legalities etc. you may entirely or give up. How many cemeteries are peppered with those who had ideas and dreams that if brought to fruition, could have positively changed and shaped the lives of so many in our society because they gave up?

Those whose lives were cut short prematurely because of various distractions or negative actions before their idea for a book, invention, business, and ministry were realized.

Jesus, as it relates to his ultimate goal, kept the end in mind. However, like it is difficult for us, it was difficult for him as well. Let us take a look. *Jesus went out as usual to the Mount of Olives, and his disciples followed him. On reaching the place, he said to them, "Pray that you will not fall into temptation." He withdrew about a stone's throw beyond them, knelt down and prayed, "Father, if you are willing, take this cup from me; yet not my will, but yours be done." An angel from heaven appeared to him and strengthened him. And being in anguish, he prayed more earnestly, and his sweat was like drops of blood falling to the ground.*

Once again, in the context of this writing; There are going to be moments that you will not want to continue with your journey. There are going to be days when the old programs of your subconscious mind will tell you, "it won't work. I digress, there are going to be days when you will have to dig deep because at times, you will be in anguish if this same Jesus was in distress about his journey don't you think you will be too?!! However, in verse 43, An angel came from heaven to strengthen him. Your angel could be in the form of your best friend, a relative, a passage in a book, a positive thought, or a program on television. Nevertheless, I AM has given you the power. (Let the weak say I AM Strong)!!

As we continue, I pray that you can see from that time to today, the human condition has not changed. As I wrote in the beginning paragraph, some of the same people that lift you up will be the same to judge and accuse you based on negative words that others may have said about you and your journey towards your success. The societal systems (priesthoods, governorships, and monarchies were threatened by the goals of one man and the participants of those systems, created enough doubt among the people to initiate a public outcry to try to stop him from succeeding.

Matthew 27:22-23 reads...

"What shall I do, then, with Jesus, who is called the Messiah?"
Pilate asked.

They all answered, "Crucify him!"

"Why? What crime has he committed?" asked Pilate.

But they shouted all the louder, "Crucify him!"

Let us continue to Matthew 27:41-44. *In the same way, the chief priests, the teachers of the law and the elders mocked him. "He saved others," they said, "but he can't save himself! He's the king of Israel! Let him come down now from the cross, and we will believe in him. 43 He trusts in God. Let God rescue him now if he wants him, for he said, 'I am the Son of God.' "In the same way, the rebels who were crucified with him also heaped insults on him.*

Once again viewing from our human condition, this is enough to make one give up on her or his journey to success. the scourge of people who will laugh at your manuscript, throw your audition video back to you, mock your physical condition, reject your applications, and say that 'you have taken this test too many times it's not for you.' So, friend, I want to ask you again how far you're willing to go for your cause if you believe and know that it will positively change the world around you?

The people in the time of Jesus thought death would end his goals they felt if they beat him beyond recognition, spit on him, scream and yell at him it would stop his success. Even the public officials who lined up along the road to witness what they thought was his last walk could not look at him with a naked eye and definitely could not fathom that He (Jesus was still on the road to success.) Each painful step that he took that day was a step in the right direction. Matthew 28: 5-7 reveals…

The angel said to the women, "Do not be afraid, for I know that you are looking for Jesus, who was crucified. He is not here; he has risen, just as he said. Come and see the place where he lay. Then go quickly and tell his disciples: 'He has risen from the dead and is going ahead of you into Galilee. There you will see him.' Now I have told you."

It may not seem that way to others, and it may look like you're taking a beating it just means that your one step closer to your blessings Verse 6 of the passage above states that He has risen, just as he Said. Friend, you can and will succeed just like the I AM said. I believe that you have to think and say it too. I don't know where you are on your journey right now. Please do not let your ideas and dreams fall prey to the world around you. I encourage and dare you today to go further.

"It is the apathetic person that sees the cause while the charitable person sees the need."

-Shannon Adler

I realize that for most of us getting up to go to work every day, whether it is your own business, or you are working for someone else can be a challenge. For some, their authentic success may come within their passion for making his or her present occupation a pleasant experience despite daily obstacles. Some are in their positions just to make ends meet and the compass of their authentic success points in another direction. In an article titled "More Than Job Satisfaction" written for the American Psychological Association by Kirsten Weir, an eye-opening discovery is made. "

Unfortunately, meaningful work may not be the norm. According to State of the American Workplace, a new report by Gallup Inc., only 30 percent of the U.S. workforce is engaged in their work — in other words, they're passionate about their work and feel strongly committed to their companies. The remaining 70 percent of American workers are either "not engaged" or "actively disengaged" in their work." The article continues speaking about those who just go to their jobs with a lack of interest. They are more likely to sew discord among colleagues and customers/clients and even steal from their place of employment. We can assuredly tie this researched behavior with parts of scripture that gives insight on how to behave within the confines of a job, volunteer work, and business.

Galatians 6:9 reads… So, let us not get tired of doing what is good. At just the right time, we will reap a harvest of blessing if we don't give up.

Colossians 3:23-24 states that… Whatever you do, work at it with all your heart, as working for the Lord, not for human masters, since you know that you will receive an inheritance from the Lord as a reward. It is the Lord Christ you are serving.

I believe that everyone on this planet searches for their path to individual success based on the shape of their world view. According to Michael G. Pratt, a professor at Boston College. "An academic might find value in scholarship, for instance. But a firefighter might look at an academic and ask, 'Are you helping people daily? If not, it's not worthwhile to work at all." The first definition of work (Noun) is 'Activity involving mental or physical effort done to achieve a purpose or result.' The (verb) 'Be engaged in physical or mental activity to achieve a purpose or result, especially in one's job; do work.

With these definitions, there are a lot of questions and maybe some pushback. First question, are you working towards your own purpose or someone else's? Second, what beyond getting paid is your desired result? Third, are you a slave to your occupation, or a humble servant? I definitely do not have the answers for these questions, but you do because they are personal within the context of your current occupation or pursuits. But for argument's sake, I will attempt to answer them this way.

If a person believes that his or her current rule is a tool or stepping stone to get where she or he actually desires to be, then I think the work becomes meaningful to that individual. With this answer, you have to be careful with selfish ambitions so that the people around you will not get stepped on as you move up. On the other hand, some people believe that their work is more prominent than they are and treat their vocations as a ministry.

So, I believe the bottom line as it relates to your authentic success is that one's attitude and perception will allow a person to navigate the waters of one's current occupation. However, continuous learning, either formal or informal is the key to going further.

Chapter Seven

WHAT YOU SAY

T

he tongue has the power of life and death, and those who love it will eat its fruit.

(Proverbs 18:21)

"Most of your sins are because of your tongues."- Muhammad Peace be upon him

"The tongue like a sharp knife... Kills without drawing blood."- Gautama Buddha

In this time, humanity is moving at a rapid pace as it relates to social behaviors. 'Alternative truths,' open condemnation, false accusations, and rumors. These things try to infiltrate our minds and hearts, not for our good but to keep us distracted just enough to knock you off course from your Authentic Success. Most of this starts with or without thought and is then verbalized through our mouths, texted by our fingers, or typed by our hands. So, as you start your day today or your day may have already started. Stop saying 'what you do not have.' many times we are asked questions about something, and we robotically reply 'I don't...'

"What do you want me to do for you?" Jesus asked him. The blind

man said, "Rabbi, I want to see."

(Mark 10:51)

Saying 'I don't.' is like throwing an object in the water and watching the ripples start small and then get bigger and bigger as they move away from the purpose and out into the body of water that it entered. Many will say do not put negative energy into the "Universe" or the atmosphere. However, I believe like the ocean, the Universe is a created space an object of creation and not an image of the Creator. You and I are an Image of the Creator. Therefore, our words pass the created Universe and send a direct message to the throne room of heaven/the infinite source of the Universe.

They traded the truth about God for a lie. So, they worshiped and served the things God created instead of the Creator himself, who is worthy of eternal praise! Amen.

(Romans 1:25)

In my opinion, we should not just unconsciously, hand over our created authority to the "Universe" but consciously recognize the alignment that exists between the Universe and each individual. Once this happens, you will be able to show gratitude to the presence of the I AM that is in you. The truth that the I Am, the infinite divine source, the kingdom of God lives in you has to be realized, and once it is recognized, all of the good you want to do and to have will be added to you. The principle of the above verse is not to put the cart before the horse. If you do, then the created "things" will become your idols.

The devil led him up to a high place and showed him in an instant all the kingdoms of the world. And he said to him, "I will give you all their authority and splendor; it has been given to me, and I can give it to anyone I want to. If you worship me, it will all be yours." Jesus answered, "It is written: 'Worship the Lord your God and serve him only.

(Luke 4:5-8)

The principle of the above scripture promotes that we should not give up our authority even in a time of weakness. When systems or individuals believe that they have you backed into the proverbial corner or your own intellect tells you that there is only one way out of a situation, You have to know who you are and that the power to overcome has been given to you. A quote from Gautama Buddha relates that "No one saves us but ourselves. No one can, and no one may. We must walk the path."

Now there was a day when the sons of God came to present themselves before the LORD, and Satan also came among them. The LORD said to Satan, "From where you come?" Then Satan answered the LORD and said, "From roaming about on the earth and walking around on it.

(Job 1:6-7)

Satan told the IAM in Job 1:11 ...*" But put forth Your hand now and touch all that he has; he will surely curse You to Your face."*

The enemy fear stood at the ready. Job could have allowed his circumstances to cause him to curse the I AM by adding a negative to the name of the infinite. Because you are one with this divine energy, you share the same name. If you continue to say I am weak, what will eventually happen? If you continue to say I am poor, you will remain impoverished. I believe you get the picture.

You desire and do not have, so you murder. You covet and cannot obtain, so you fight and quarrel. You do not have, because you do not ask.

(James 4:2)

Remember the LORD your God. He is the one who gives you the power to be successful, to fulfill the covenant he confirmed to your ancestors with an oath.

(Deuteronomy 8:18)

In my opinion, 'universe worship' is very suspect. Many 'self-improvements' coaches promote it as a secret or a mystery like a universe is a personal vending machine where one can dial up Health, Wealth, etc. Yes, I have personally experienced manifestations of 'things,' but I do not and cannot give credit to the Universe. Because it is the Divine presence (I AM) that lives in me, the Universe responds to. Some self-improvement analysts may say it's whatever you want to call it (Universe, God, Higher Power, etc.). A recognized scientist may argue that there is more than one universe. Science implies that people should consider being a part of a multiverse. Hold on, I am going somewhere with this because I want you to make an informed decision along your journey to authentic success.

According to Clara Moskowitz, "Scientist can't be sure what the shape of space-time is, but most likely, it's flat (as opposed to spherical even donut shape) and stretches out infinitely. But if space-time goes on forever, then it must start repeating at some point, because there are a finite number of ways particles can be arranged in space and time." On the other hand, the late Stephen Hawking and Thomas Hertog argue that the concept of eternal inflation (multiverses) is inaccurate and that there is only one universe. Hawking and Hertog go on to suggest that our Universe never had a singular moment of creation.

If there is more than one universe, and they all may appear to be slightly different, which one will respond to the laws that are said to govern the known world? Or if the Universe just sort of popped up without a dispenser of creation, who set the laws that govern it? Take a deep breath. Scientific theories and concepts about the Universe are implied and never really stated. However, there are those who seem to have personal experience and expert knowledge of the 'laws' that govern what we call the Universe. Let us examine these laws, their origins, and if they can be applied to your authentic success.

1. The Law of Divine Oneness reveals that we are interconnected with everything that is. You will know this when you realize the impact that your actions (word and deed) have on people and things around you. Remember the ripple effect of an object thrown into a body of water? You have to know and understand that this law goes into effect as soon as your eyes open to start a new day. The Shema reflects this law.

Hear, O Israel: The LORD our God, the LORD is one. You shall love the LORD your God with all your heart and with all your soul and with all you might. And these words that I command you today shall be on your heart. You shall teach them diligently to your children and shall talk of them when you sit in your house, and when you walk by the way, and when you lie down, and when you rise. You shall bind them as a sign on your hand, and they shall be as frontlets between your eyes. You shall write them on the doorposts of your house and on your gates.

Deuteronomy 6:4-9

2. The Law of Vibration relays that all matter is continually moving and broadcasting on different frequencies and carry specific levels of energy. According to Tara Mullarkey, "The quantum physicists have proven it: We are not just this physical body. Our presence doesn't end at our skin line. We have an energy field around us." To put this law into action, one must consciously recognize your right now emotional state, show compassion through acts of kindness, relax your thoughts and movements through deep breathing, show gratitude, meditate on and speak words or phrases that bring life and vitality to you and others.

#

Whatever things are true, whatever things are noble, whatever things are just, whatever things are pure, whatever things are lovely, whatever things are of good report, if there is any virtue and if there is anything praiseworthy—meditate on these

things... Phil 4:8

3. The law of correspondence relates to repeating patterns. When we slow down, we can see patterns in our lives and thoughts. These same patterns are often being replicated in other places. To activate this law, you must recognize these patterns and consciously make an effort to change them in a way that would promote a different outcome.

They said to Moses, "Was it because there were no graves in Egypt that you brought us to the desert to die? What have you done to us by bringing us out of Egypt? Exodus 14:11

Although the Egyptians were hard taskmasters, the former slaves were fearful of the change that was unfolding right before their eyes. I believe they were so afraid of this change that they seem to have regret for breaking their usual pattern. Generational patterns of poverty, adultery, alcoholism, sexual deviance, etc. Exist all around the planet. I believe if one desires any type of success in his or her life patterns must be broken. The generations of Jacob appeared to ignore the promptings and actions of the I AM and failed to see and understand the law of correspondence.

Donna Labermeier writes, "No doubt you're aware of the expressions, "As Above, So Below," or "On Earth, as it is in Heaven." Well, these ideas pertain to the line of communication, or correspondence, between the lower energies of the physical mind (Earth) and the higher powers of the Divine Mind (Heaven). The key to changing your physical reality is by realizing that you are more of a spiritual being than a physical one. Every step you take in your physical life reflects the spiritual self that is trying to be realized, which is why lessons are repeated in our lives over and over again until we learn them."

4. The law of attraction promotes frequency and vibration in the context of lining up with things and people that have the same frequencies and vibrations. If you're a positive person, you will attract everything positive towards you. If you are negative, you will continue to attract negative things. This law, like all of the others, is not centered in the created Universe. It is centered within the I AM that lives in you because you are created in the image of the "I AM."I encourage you to read First John 4:2-4. This law is not a secret. It only remains a secret to those who do not apply it. Proverbs 23:7 is widely used as an example of this law. However, when reading it in its full context, it speaks of a frugal person who is always thinking about the cost of things because their generosity is not sincere. If a person thinking is so narrow that he or she is still thinking about the value of things, they will never attract what they desire. The law of attraction is activated by faith, which promotes persistence to gain your desired result.

If I can create a formula for the law of attraction, it probably would be A=F(P) Attraction equals faith time persistence. Let us prove this concept. Earl Nightingale writes, "We become what we think about. A person who is thinking about a real and worthwhile goal is going to reach it because that's what he's thinking about.

Conversely, the person who has no goal, who doesn't know where he's going, and whose thoughts must, therefore, be thoughts of confusion, anxiety, fear, and worry will thereby create a life of frustration, fear, anxiety, and worry. And if he thinks about nothing ... he becomes nothing." The carpenter from Nazareth left us with a story and a declaration that further lends to the existence of the law of attraction.

Then Jesus said to them, "Suppose you have a friend, and you go to him at midnight and say, 'Friend, lend me three loaves of bread; a friend of mine on a journey has come to me, and I have no food to offer him.' And suppose the one inside answers, 'Don't bother me. The door is already locked, and my children and I are in bed. I can't get up and give you anything.' I tell you, even though he will not get up and give you the bread because of friendship, yet because of your shameless audacity, he will surely get up and give you as much as you need.

"So I say to you: Ask, and it will be given to you; seek, and you will find; knock, and the door will be opened to you.

Luke 11:5-9

5. The Law of Inspired action is interwoven with the law of attraction. For this law to be activated, you must have a goal and a plan on how that goal will be reached. Earl Nightingale writes, "People with goals succeed because they know where they're going. It's that simple. Failures, on the other hand, believe that their lives are shaped by circumstances ... by things that happen to them ... by outside forces."

For I know the plans I have for you," declares the Lord, "plans to prosper you and not to harm you, plans to give you hope and a future.

Jeremiah 29:11

6. The Law of Perpetual Transmutation of Energy; Here is a simple example of how this law works. You walk into a room in a happy mood. However, the people in the room are putting off negative vibrations, and you can actually feel them. Let's say you remain in that room for a while their low vibrations could possibly interrupt your high (happy vibration) and your happy mood swings to a somber one. Talk about a buzz kill. However, in a one-on-one situation, the High frequency (happy, positive person) will most likely trigger an energy transformation that will brighten the room.

7. The Law of Cause and Effect. We can see and understand how this law takes effect in the physical realm, but what about the spiritual? Are we mindful of this law when it comes to our thoughts? Do we realize effects, negative or positive can manifest because of our thoughts? The I AM warns us about how this law can steer you in the wrong direction if you are not mindful of its existence.

The heart is deceitful above all things. And beyond cure. Who can understand it? "I the Lord search the heart. and examine the mind, to reward each person according to their conduct, according to what their deeds deserve.

Jeremiah 17:9-10

The subconscious mind can be tricky because it is active all of the time. Buried negative notions and thoughts can resurface if we do not consciously recognize them and reprogram them. "Everything in life comes from the ideas in your mind." So, our thoughts are manifested into words and words hold power. To lend confirmation to this idea, Scientist has conducted experiments based on Genesis chapter 1:1-3 when the I AM said "Let there be Light," and light appeared. Samuel J. Hunt has conducted experiments backed by proven research that the infinite source of energy (God) sent a sonic influence over the waters basically creating light.

Researched documentation and the analyses validate Hunts theories in his "Episteme Scientia, the Law of all that is." In his abstract, Hunt states that "An examination of the sequential mathematical and experimental dual proof of the Genesis record of origins underlying the institution of all that is in the universe – from waves to matter to the mind."

Your situation can change by the sound of your voice. Dr. Eikerenkoetter puts it this way. "Now let me tell you something about these words, "I AM." They are powerful. In fact, "I AM" is the most powerful affirmation you can make. Why? Because every time you say, "I AM," you are announcing the God presence and the God Power within you."

Chapter Eight

SEE-P-THREE-OH

T he title of this chapter is a cheesy play on the name of one of my favorite movie characters. However, I believe that it speaks to the elements that all of us need to achieve 'authentic success' We have to seek and see opportunities that are tailored for the talents that each one of us have been blessed to have. Next, we have to incorporate the 3 P's. Prayer, Persistence, and Patience. The 'Oh' stands for what I call those light bulb moments.

When talking to people, discerning situations, their outcomes, and creating a 'win-win.' All of these things also depend on our level of maturity and our upbringing. From the age of five, I knew I wanted to lead and help others. For me, growing up was not without adversity. However, I definitely cannot boast about myself. It was and still is the power of the "I AM" that gets me through each day.

In previous chapters, I have stated that it is your 'right now thoughts' that matter. I believe this action definitely has to be practiced via 'See-P-three-0h' I will share an example from my life. I am still recovering from open heart surgery, which included insertion of a VAD or LVAD (Left Ventricular Assist Device). As you can imagine, this was and is a drastic change for my family.

However, if I keep my thoughts on the past, thinking about how I got to this point, I can possibly sink into a state of depression, which would stop my healing process. Or I could focus on my future with the LVAD constantly questioning my health options as time passes. This could put me in a state of anxiety that could also hinder my healing process. So, I choose to focus on my right now thoughts and actions. Right now, I am working on this chapter, it is a beautiful and breezy sunny Sunday afternoon, and I am in a state of gratitude as I am also enjoying the conversation between my wife and daughter about homework.

So, with all of that said, I am going to share extensive examples of people in our modern society who have learned how to achieve the success that is authentic to them and share their journey with others. My challenge to you is to recognize 'See-P-Three-Oh' in their formulas for success and make them your own. But first, I need to attend to a little housekeeping. Earl Nightingale shared in his radio broadcast "The Strangest Secret" that "A success is anyone who is realizing a predetermined worthy ideal because that's what he or she decided to do… deliberately. But only one out of 20 does that! The rest are "failures."

If the rest are "failures," could it be that setting and achieving small goals within a success framework could decrease the number of those who fail? According to the American Psychological Association, those who teach self-development should be aware of popular myths about immediately changing someone's behavior as it relates to successfully meeting goals. "Habit and behavior change are hard, but with some insight and techniques from recent studies, helping clients move from goal intentions to successful completion can be done."

I have had the pleasure of reading and experienced goal achieving results from a writing called "It Works." By RHJ. Needless to say, when I was first introduced to this writing, I was skeptical, but since it was only a few pages long, I dove in. Stop wishing and start believing I believe is the main idea of this writing. The book speaks about a 'power' so close that it is discounted, and its function is so simple that the concept is difficult to understand. This book was introduced in 1926 and is still relative today. Science, psychology, and theology may appear not to agree with the instructions outlined for achieving one's goals. However, from my personal experience, it does work.

This book recognizes that there is a power within each individual that will complete a perfect work that is seen by the objective mind and can be carried out by the subjective mind when it comes into alignment with the 'I AM' that is within you. So, what does it mean to think objectively? It involves discerning the facts in a situation, the circumstances that surround it and making the best possible decision for a beneficial outcome. However, that is easier said than done. Past experiences, the emotions attached to them, and our so-called 'expert knowledge' can cloud our objectivity.

I believe our objectivity is often challenged by sales reps, advertisements, and even our own embedded habits, trying to get us to react immediately. The terms; *there are only a few left in stock, act now,* or *this offer is only suitable for today.* If we really pay attention, these calls to action are placed on us in different forms every day either at home, work, vacation, or shopping. I remember the cartoons where the devil is on one shoulder and the angel on the other pitching their ideas of how one should respond to a given situation.

"The reality is we all have biases. If they're not managed, we then may pay in lost opportunities, money, relationships, and other ways, says Elizabeth R. Thornton, professor of management practice at Babson College in Boston." In the book "It Works," the author puts it this way. "Your objective mind and will are so vacillating that you usually only wish for things and the wonderful, capable power within you does not function." So, if the rational mind (conscience) only wishes to have what it observes what about the subconscious mind? Brian Tracy puts it this way. "Your subconscious mind is an unquestioning servant that works day and night to make your behavior fit a pattern consistent with your emotionalized thoughts, hopes, and desires. Your subconscious mind grows either flowers or weeds in the garden of your life, whichever you plant by the mental equivalents you create. "In "It Works," the author claims that there is a power in us that can give us what we truly desire.

This 'Power' who the author calls Emmanuel an I call the "I

AM" is able and available to manifest the desires of our rational mind. So, you're probably asking, which one is it the objective or subjective perception? I believe that it is both. To put it only if I can, this concept is not unlike a restaurant where you look at the menu and see the food and drink you desire to have. You order it (conscious mind), and your order (the picture or the description of that food item) goes into the kitchen which you cannot see, to be processed (sub-conscience mind). As if by magic, what you ordered from the menu, the picture that you saw or the description that you read is sitting in front of you ready to be eaten. Larry Crawford answers the question this way. "Consciousness is a brain function. The brain being objective and the role being subjective.

In the Book "It Works," the author gives a practical plan for the reader to follow. I have developed this plan, and I am a witness that the reader who makes this plan a committed goal will benefit from it. When one compares thought with the speed of light science discovered that human thought travels at a rate of 186,000 miles per second. This means one single thought travels 930,000 times faster than our voice. Reverend Willie F. Wilson states (paraphrased) that whatever we habitually think (ruling state of mind) sinks down into our subconscious mind where the power of the "I AM" resides in us then creates according to the disposition of our emotions. It is safe to say your success is truly authentic to you and your feelings. Therefore, it (your present state of mind) can have a positive or negative effect on you and the people around you.

As you already know, the road to your 'authentic success' is not going to be easy. It is good to be aware of a pitfall that is simple to run into if you do not become cognitively aware of its existence. You have to remind yourself that human behavior is driven by a need to avoid pain and gain pleasure. This "need" can easily be manipulated by others to achieve compliance. For example, a lower order needs like safety can be threatened by asking a person, "Are you sure that you will be able to survive without this five-figure income? If a person yields to this manipulation, he or she may never take the opportunity to explore their dreams of starting a business because the spirit of doubt was triggered in your subconscious mind and the business that may have been a blessing to many will never come into existence. Take note, the subconscious mind operates on impressions which the conscious mind has forgotten.

The next writing, we will explore is "Prosperity How to Attract It: Living a life of financial freedom, conquer debt, increase income, and maximize wealth" by Dr. Orison Swett Marden. It is peculiar how our human condition when it comes to prosperity, never really changes.

In the book, Dr. Marden talks about how he has interviewed many people who he called "timid" and asked them why they allowed opportunities to pass by them. The answers vary from lack of courage, lack of confidence in oneself, or believing that you are not worthy enough to seek a position so far above your current station. This is not just lacking self-confidence; this is a person who does not trust him or herself.

Marden writes; "This shrinking, this timidity or self-effacement, often proves a worse enemy to success than actual incompetence." I believe that this is a person who is not at peace with him or herself. I will discuss this in detail later in the book. Marden has a chapter entitled "Getting Aroused" Please do not allow your subconscious to give you a thought and picture about this title (even though I know it already has) without placing it within the context of success. I believe Marden is asking what is your heart's desire or what motivates you enough to stimulate an attitude of success? He makes this suggestion. "Whatever you do in life, make any sacrifice necessary to keep in an ambition arousing atmosphere, an environment that will stimulate you to self-development. Keep close to people who understand you, who believe in you, who will help you discover yourself and encourage you to make the most of yourself."

So, what does all of this have to do with my Authentic Success? If you are reading this right now you may be thinking; Show me the part about where I can make a lot of money because the pictures that pop up in my mind whenever success is mentioned are peppered with visions of money.

I am going to get to that later. However, if you do not come to know the real and whole you, the money will flow in and out of your hands like water, and you will never be able to hold on to it. Let me ask you the reader this question. What do you believe about yourself? This is a question that practitioners in the field of personal development either fail to ask. They imply instead of stating facts, or they hope you figure it out after you leave their seminar, "church service," or business rally. What do you believe about yourself? I would like you to meditate on this question write some things down and revisit your plans for achieving your goals. Another question to ask yourself is, "What do I say to myself about myself?"

There is another chapter in Marden's writing that is titled "Had Money but Lost It." I believe the essence of this chapter has one message and that is if you guard your heart and mind it will be difficult for outside forces to take your money from you or for you to blindly hand it over without discerning what you want or need is at the time. Systems (Banks, insurance companies, and retail conglomerates) are gaining immense wealth and real power on the "Ignorance of the Masses. The "I AM" revealed this to the prophet Hosea in chapter 4:6 take a few minutes to read it for yourself.

Rejecting knowledge or ignoring the fact that the power of the infinite resides in your conscious and subconscious mind can be detrimental to your authentic success. Why? Because you fail to understand how this power works, give up on learning more about it, and allow others to think on your behalf or in other words, give up your authority. That makes you subject to the psychological manipulation written in Dan Crosby's book "Psychological Triggers" chapter 3 "Needs: The Game Changer."

For the theologian who is reading this, you may understand it if I use the biblical illustration of giving up your birthright (Genesis 25:29-34). Marden states how the corporate world treats those who reject the "I AM" "The schemer's bank on it that it is easy to swindle people who do not know how to protect their property. They thrive on the ignorance of their fellows. They know that a shrewd advertisement, a cunningly worded circular, a hypnotic appeal will bring the hard earnings of these unsuspecting people out of hiding-places into their own coffers."

Let's take a look at the "Wealth Choice" by Dennis Kimbrough. I believe the overarching theme of this book is having a mindset rooted in faith. Remember the questions earlier in this chapter. I recommended you ask yourself. Kimbrough puts it this way in the context of money." Without considering temporary setbacks and extraordinary fortunes of inheritance or luck, if you wish to know how average individuals feel about themselves, look at their bank accounts. Money, or the lack thereof, is the most crucial measurement of your mindset." Amos Winbush Owner of CyberSynchs, believes that a person who has a desire to achieve success should ask themselves, "What is my purpose? What are my true gifts? Never allow what you can't do to stop you from doing what you can do."

In Robert Kiyosaki's video, "You are Programmed to Be Poor," he reveals what he believes is a weak indictment on our educational system. That indictment is that our educational system does not teach about money. The interviewer asked that until you change your mindset that money won't help you." Kiyosaki agrees, he states, "If you are poor you will always be poor because the money will disappear that fast."

Kiyosaki goes on to say that the poor blame the rich and the government for their circumstance and agrees that the "poor mindset" is passed down genetically. Now, I do not and will not submit to that belief. However, I do believe that it is a learned behavior. Some of the oldest religious denominations have purposely programmed a poverty mindset into other cultures during centuries of so-called conversion. In turn, the poverty mindset is passed down as a psychological inheritance from family member to a family member. This is the kicker, no matter if the family is rich or poor. If hell and damnation (religious dogma) are programmed into the sub-conscience of a loved one or if a parent or other family member regularly speak negative words (You can't... you will never... or you are just like you are no good...). The odds are high that the person on the receiving end will have a "poor mindset." Kiyosaki goes on to say that "It's (poor mindset) in their words and their words become flesh. But when they say, 'I can't afford it,' or 'I can't do that!' they go down they become what they say."

I believe this chapter has opened up the oh in 'SEE-Three-P-OH' because this is not a cookie cutter success formula. As you continue reading, one of the overarching themes to authentic success is "you become what you say." This is not a religious mandate, but it is part of a law or a principle that is directly attached to the human condition. In this chapter, I have included several statements and opinions, both old and supposedly new from other personal development leaders and authors. I ask you to go back and listen to or read their philosophies about success so you can make an informed decision about your own authentic success.

Chapter Nine

R.E.N.E.W.

H ave you ever heard the statement 'I had to reinvent myself '? I believe those who make such statements, have resolved to get rid of a piece or pieces of their character that he or she believes is holding them back from the desired goal. However, to come to such resolve, he or she must have had an opportunity for a time of self-reflection. There is a science behind self-reflection that indicates a mindful awareness of ones being and his or her reactions to past situations.

For example, you are probably thinking about something that you should not have said or done to another individual either in the context of defending yourself and your position or just speaking your mind with filters off. Research states that "A sense of self is a collection of schemata regarding one's abilities, traits and attitudes that guides our behaviors, choices and social interactions. The accuracy of one's sense of self will impact the ability to function effectively in the world.

"With self-reflection comes the "R-word" and when people hear it, it sets off a stream of emotions that are either for it or against it. Whether you like it or not; it is something that I believe must be done before, during, and after your successful goals are achieved. This word, if used rightly, can and will free your mind and help you to live a prosperous life. I will provide you with its definitions within the context of this book. "

A change of mind" and "regret/remorse." Repentance is a necessary emotional response for one to achieve what I call authentic success. Notice I stated for 'authentic success.' There are many who we see as materially "successful" that steamroll over this quality like it does not exist. Maybe you have a colleague, friend, boss, or relative that will just do, for lack of a better word 'stuff' that hurts others emotionally and sometimes physically without a second thought. There is a psychological explanation for that type of behavior, but this is the wrong book for that.

"How queer everything is today! And yesterday things went on just as usual. I wonder if I've been changed in the night. Let me think: was I the same when I got up this morning? I almost think I can remember feeling a little different. But, if I'm not the same, the next question is, "Who in the world am I?" Ah, that's the great puzzle!"

(Lewis Carroll, 1678.)

Although some of this is covered in chapter one. Knowing who you are, your limits, expectations, weaknesses, faults, likes, dislikes, etc. Comes into the circle of your authentic success. However, If you can reconcile with and recognize the "I Am" within you, there is a possibility that the "puzzle" can be solved. You're probably saying to yourself, 'what the heck is he talking about?' I am talking about accountability. After self-examination, can you take ownership of the things you don't like about yourself and push forward?

N.B.A. celebrity Byron Scott and marketing professional/business owner Charles Norris in their book "Slam-Dunk Success" share an example of self-reflection with N.B.A. players who were coached by Mr. Scott. Coach Scott had to bench a couple of star players that were not playing well at the time. If you get an opportunity to read their book, you will learn about the character of Mr. Scott and how he has a desire to see people do well and become successful in life.

However, it was a challenge for him getting through to these two athletes. Mr. Norris offered this advice. "Ask them, 'what's blocking you from being great? And see how they respond." Mr. Norris then took it a little further saying, "After they answer, ask them, 'How can I help you get there?" After Mr. Scott posed these questions to the athletes, self-reflection was almost immediate. The athletes shared their thoughts with coach Scott, and one of the gentlemen believed that he needed someone to hold him accountable. Coach Scott accepted and embraced the offer. Fostering successful change in the player's lives and their organization.

Examine me, O LORD, and try me; Test my mind and my heart. (Psalm 26:2).

The Psalmist recognized that accountability is necessary for self-improvement. This is not a religious statement but a part of our human condition. With that in mind, on your way to success; you have to be Resilient, Encouraged, Nourishing, have Endurance, and be Well informed **(R.E.N.E.W.)**. Being resilient is actually more complicated than one would think. I believe every human possess resiliency, but to what degree? Dr. Stephen Southwick states that "Determinants of resilience include a host of biological, psychological, social and cultural factors that interact with one another to determine how one respond to stressful experiences."

One of my daughter's is graduating from college this year and has aspirations to attend medical school. From a parent's point of view, I get a little nervous because she is holding down three jobs one full-time at a hospital and she is always on the go with her sorority and other efforts. She sometimes calls when she does not do well on a test, or there is drama in the workplace and expresses how tired she is. However, when I recommend rest or even cutting loose an activity or job, she will not do it. However, for a 20-year-old college student who is determined to achieve a level of success, I believe this is a stressful position to be in.

Dr. Gregg Henriques writes," It is neither an exaggeration nor is it alarmist to claim that there is a mental health crisis facing America's college students. Evidence suggests that this group has higher levels of stress and psychopathology than at any time in the nation's history." The good news is that there are students who can overcome these experiences. Because of resiliency, we have many writers, ancient and modern who can write and share their experiences of how they were able to master their thoughts in stressful circumstances, allow their success to become something greater than themselves and share it with the world.

College grads, housewives, entrepreneurs, blue collar, white collar, and everyone in-between can attest to the stress of life itself. However, it is the ability to persevere in difficult situations that will keep you on a successful path. I had a college professor who always told me that 'excuses are tools of incompetence' He only needed to say to me that one time. After my first failing grade in that class, I understood the saying. I wonder if those who we can call authentically successful ever made excuses on their journey to success. I believe that one can become resilient because she or he can persevere through their circumstances without excuses. On your journey to success, you may be seen as a(n) misunderstood genius, eccentric, noble, or even insane. Regardless of the labels that are thrust upon you, the divine gift of perseverance that is available to you cannot be questioned.

Most of us had heard and quoted this unofficial definition of insanity" to do what you have always done and expect different results" The experts are not exactly sure when this famous phrase was coined or its author. However, in-spite of public opinion this particular sentence can possibly delay or stifle your success. How is that? First, one must recognize the word insanity as a legal term, not psychological. Ryan Howes Ph.D., A.B.P.P. has this to say about the phrase. "I'm not in the habit of slamming cute sayings, but I think there's a dark underbelly to this one.

I've started hearing people use it in the service of avoidance, which is a defense mechanism. Rather than facing their fears, they grab on to this saying for protection against possible failure, pain, or rejection." Second, you can't use this sentence in the same context as perseverance. It will be like mixing water with oil. When used in the correct context, the phrase alludes to perseveration where a person's efforts are discouraging, inefficient, and uncontrollable. "Perseverance is a strong, valuable quality. Perseveration is a troubling issue needing clinical attention. Don't let a quaint saying blur this distinction."

Let us complete the rest of this acrostic (R.E.N.E.W.). As you begin to explore the depths of resiliency as it relates to your authentic success. I would like for you to be encouraged along your journey. Often you are so busy helping others, that you find there is little to no encouragement for you. So, what does research tells us about encouragement? The Father of Alderman psychology Alfred Adler studied the social constructs of encouragement and considered encouragement to be an integral part of our human condition. An Adlerian psychotherapist noted that "to provide encouragement is to inspire or help others, particularly toward a conviction that they can work on finding solutions and that they can cope with any predicament."

Through his research on encouragement Y. Joel Wong reminds us that the act of encouragement is broad and includes verbal and non-verbal gestures. For example, a teacher might give a head nod and a smile to a student who is progressing on a lesson, a person may show a thumbs up or a pat on the back in a sporting competition. I believe it is beneficial to your authentic success to take a broad and narrow approach when it comes to encouraging others. So, it is helpful for you to accept encouragement when it comes your way.

I give credit to the Alderian school of thought. However, I Am created us to accept encouragement and to encourage each other. The unknown author of the letter to the Hebrews which is speculated to be written in A.D. 70 appears to empathize with the woes of society during that period, by giving words of encouragement that are still embraced today. *"But encourage one another daily, as long as it is called Today, so that none of you may be hardened by sin's deceitfulness," Hebrews 3:13*

Nourishing could be synonymous with encouragement. However, as it is related to your authentic success, it lends to the health of your success. Are you reading, practicing, networking, and devoting time to your goal? I believe in keeping the dream alive, you have to feed it. Yes, faith is always at the forefront of our success. Therefore, one must faithfully nourish (work) the field to harvest a stellar crop. Kathy Caption writes, "But never sacrifice your future self. Find ways to plant the seeds for your future self every day, by building skills, strengths, and experience in directions that will enliven you."

Chapter Ten

CLEAN UP

Your authentic success can and should be a lasting success, not just in terms of material wealth but a long-lasting inheritance that will continue to bless others long past your time in the land of the living. Your authentic success is driven by your thoughts, and you have read about various forms of success throughout this book. I have listened to and understood a plethora of materials as it relates to success, be it religious, secular, in-between, and the scientific. However, I have found that most of the religious content fails to clarify the idea that the power they call God lives in all of us. For many of them, "God" is only an external source.

I believe that some of the secular teachings place too much of an emphasis on "dialing up the universe" and not enough on working with the whole individual in terms of forgiveness first of oneself, then others. Unfortunately, without mercy, I guarantee your success will not last as the "universe" will spit you out. Now there is what I call the in-between those personal developers who use ancient principles and secular techniques. I find most of them are cautious about using repentance as it may be too religious for some and strike a tone of judgment in the minds of those who subscribe to their teachings. Now the scientist (credentialed experts) who claim to have mapped the human brain, and its multiple functions fail to understand the simplicity of the human condition, the zeal of the human spirit, and the enthusiasm that lies within.

It is a given that no one has all the answers about how to achieve your authentic success because everyone teaches it based on their own success. In this book, I have given a view of a few modalities that can lead you to your authentic success. Now it is up to you the reader to make an informed decision about which path you should take.

I have found that the study of conscience and subconscious thought has been around since the establishment of the kingdoms and tribes in the Nile Valley long before the establishment of organized religion. Our ancestors did not have new explanations for their understanding of the infinite power we call "God." However, in this time, we are fortunate to embrace and expand our knowledge of the infinite based on the close relationship and understanding some of our ancestors had of this infinite power. It is comforting to know and understand that this creative power is present in you and me right now.

As we have read from various other writings, it is a recognizable fact that there is an energy that amplifies our thoughts, and when our beliefs align with this perpetual energy, things happen. The proof is all around you. The city that you live in, the cars you drive, the clothes you wear, all came from an individual or collective thought(s). We can see this in the ancient story of the tower of Babel you can read it in its entirety in the book of beginnings, chapter 11 verses 1-9:

And the Lord came down to see the city and the tower which the children of men built. And the Lord said, "Behold, the people are one, and they have all one language, and this they begin to do; and now nothing will be withheld from them which they have imagined doing."

Imagination in the English means "faculty of the mind which forms and manipulates images. The Hebrew translation yester "a shaping, "hence, a thought" I believe that from this information, you can draw your own conclusion about thoughts being manifested into the material world. However, I think in this story, human thought was not aligned with the divine view because the story reflects that the city was being built not to help others but to show social power and might.

A take away from this story is; running on your own steam will not produce lasting results. Another take away is that your imagination is a thought shaping process.   Visualizing your goals are essential and fun. Using your minds-eye to actually see what you want to be, do, and have, programs those goals into your subconscious mind and manifest those things into existence. This brings into understanding the words of the teacher in the book of Matthew, chapter six, verse four. *"Thy Father who seeth in secret shall reward thee openly."* The power of the "I AM" that is within you aligns with your desires in your mind (secret place), and those desires become tangible so that everyone can see them.

Dr. Frederick J. Eikerenkoetter states that "The subconscious mind in you is always being impressed, it is still recording, and it does not forget. He also describes the word heart as it is used in religious text as the deep subconscious level of the individual mind. According to Lipton, the conscious mind is limited and can only handle a few tasks. However, the subconscious mind can perform thousands of functions at the same time. Modern science recently discovered that it is the unconscious mind that really shapes our decisions and our lives. Neuroscientist found that we are conscious of only about 5% of our cognitive activity. For most of us, only 1% of our day is spent using the conscious mind the rest comes from the subconscious mind.

To clarify this, a person really has to work hard intentionally and purposefully to reprogram his or her subconscious. Authentic success requires that a person works on themselves first. Like I have written before real forgiveness can reprogram the subconscious along with other useful techniques. With that said, we can read and understand Romans as it relates to the mind. Chapter 12, verses 2-3 (NLV). "Don't copy the behavior and customs of this world, but let God transform you into a new person by changing the way you think. Then you will learn to know God's will for you, which is good and pleasing and perfect. Verse 3 second sentence. "Be honest in your evaluation of yourself, measuring yourself by the faith God has given us.

First of all, if we view what we call "God" as just an outside source, a change of thinking will never happen. One has to realize and believe the divine power is in you and begin to reprogram (transform your way of thinking) the Bible gives us a clue on how to do it. Philippians chapter 4, verse 8, reads, *"And now, dear brothers and sisters, one final thing. Fix your thoughts on what is true, and honorable, and right, and pure, and lovely, and admirable. Think about things that are excellent and worthy of praise.* When put in its proper context (the mind) This is not religious mumbo jumbo it is a genuine part of our human condition. I believe that our thoughts and feelings should always point toward healthy living, personal happiness, loving relationships (including yourself) success in your vocation, prosperity be it material or non-material and the ability to use the money to bring forth the good that you desire

To put reprograming the subconscious into practice, one must go beyond the power of positive thinking. Positive thinking works when a belief that is imprinted in the psyche aligns with our creative mind (conscience). For example, the religious faith of drinking deadly poison and snake handling works because there is an alignment between the artistic soul and the divine mind (subconscious).

The surrounding religious belief of the poison drinking congregants that "you are not holy enough to drink poison and survive" or "God did not find you worthy" is not accurate. This brings to light the passage located in the gospel of Mark Chapter 9 verse 23 (NIV) "If you can?" said Jesus. *"Everything is possible for one who believes."* Read the story in context Mark 9:22-24. I shared in the introduction that we should not stop and worship or hold in reverence the personalities ancient or modern that deliver messages of law and principle. They, (those personalities) are doorways or gates that we should walk through to gain precise knowledge and understanding about how these principles and laws operate. However, many will not obtain a life-changing knowledge of how it all works because their right now thoughts are being drowned out by the noise of the world. As K-12 educators. My wife and I are always saddened by the fact that many children, as well as adults, struggle with reading and comprehension. Most of the children and adults that we encounter have been labeled by systems as having a reading deficiency.

I have found that most of these people are deficient in the area of belief. I will try to explain it this way. First if one believes others definition of you the subconscious mind especially that of a child will hold on to the negative diagnosis My wife has tutored children second graders as a matter of fact, whose parents have been told by the system that the child had a reading disorder.

The parents that consult with my wife are the parents who do not take the evaluation the system gave their child as gospel and seek outside help. My wife has had unprecedented success with the children she tutors in the areas of reading because now they (the children) believe that they can read and enjoy doing it. As a result, the children's confidence and test scores skyrocket. Unfortunately, some parents and teachers do not consciously realize that they could very well be the reason why their child or student has a reading deficiency. Now imagine the later taken to the umpteenth power (figure of speech) that means there are masses of people who do not have the privilege to exercise the free, powerful, and creative gift of reading.

To place this within the context of this book, how can one align with the power of the "I AM" and gain real life-giving success if he or she cannot read or comprehend? I believe this is an esoteric principle of Hosea Chapter 4 and Verse 6: *My people are destroyed from lack of knowledge. "Because you have rejected knowledge, I also reject you as my priests; because you have ignored the law of your God, I also will ignore your children.*

The above statement may have been written many millennia ago, but it applies to the right now. Parents are the priest of their homes and are given the responsibility to mold the minds of their children. Children cannot know and purposely apply their creative power without positive guidance and being told that they can be, do, and have the good that they desire according to the good that the law is. If the knowledge of the I AM is not read and understood by individuals, the "world mind" takes over and does the thinking for them.

I believe that the Bible and other ancient compilations are esoteric in nature the Teacher from Nazareth puts it this way about having a successful and abundant life. In Luke Chapter 13 Verse 24: *"Strive to enter through the narrow door. For many, I tell you, will seek to enter and will not be able.* Matthew Chapter 7, Verse 14 reads *but small is the gate and narrow the road that leads to life, and only a few find it.* Now, let us take a look at a few techniques that you can use to ignite the power of the "I AM" that lives in you.

REPETITION

Being an educator for over twenty years, I have learned that repetition is the surest way to reprogram the old thoughts in your subconscious mind. However, repetition takes work and discipline. Every personal development book that you have read and video that you have watched contains curriculum that gives at least a 30-day challenge to put a particular system to the test. Some of the processes of repetition are...

JOURNALING

Writing down your goals and desires for your authentic and scheduling a time to read them every day. I suggest In the mornings after you give praises to the "I AM" for seeing another day read your journal before you look at the news, traffic report, etc. You want to consciously start your day with positive information that came from your own creative mind, not someone else's. After you give thanks to the Infinite for another day, reread your journal right before you go to bed. Try to stay away from the nightly news before you go to bed, lousy news travels, and it goes straight to your subconscious mind.

VISUALIZATION

Dr. Eikerenkoetter states that. "Only when you have a clear idea of what you want will you get it. Deciding what you want is the first step in creating it." You have to see yourself being, doing, and having the good that you desire. Remember to include yourself in your visions. See and feel yourself healthy, on vacation, driving the vehicle you want, or having the money to start a successful business that will bless you and others. Visualize yourself as already having it. Go to a quiet place where you feel comfortable to close your physical eyes and open the mind's eye. Remember to smile during your visualization because what you are visualizing should make you happy.

AFFIRMATIONS

Repeating positive affirmations daily is another sure-fire way to reprogram the subconscious mind. No matter your culture, there is a positive affirmation for you. Prayer is affirming self-conscious oneness with the "I AM" within you, and the Infinite is fulfilling every good and perfect work in you. (Prayer is not just for when you're in trouble) It is one thing to say it, it is another thing to believe it. You have to believe without a doubt what you say. I think this is the principle of Isaiah 26:3 *You will keep in perfect peace all who trust in you, all whose thoughts are fixed on you!* Repeating this affirmation. I AM Health, I AM Happiness, I AM Love I AM Success, and I AM Prosperity will start you on the way to your authentic success.

GIVING and RECEIVING

Money is essential for us to maneuver in the land of the living. It seems that when people are legally receiving payment from any source, few complain. However, when it comes time to give, there always seem to be hesitation, frustration, and criticism. I have learned that people do not need money; however, money needs them to do the good that you desire to be done, want, and have. Stop feeling guilty and shame for having or not having it. Because money needs you and will come to you if you ask it to. The

Prophet Jesus demonstrates this in Matthew 17:27, as the temple taxes required to be paid. "*However, not to give offense to them, go to the sea and cast a hook and take the first fish that comes up, and when you open its mouth, you will find a shekel. Take that and give it to them for yourself and for me.*"

Most of us are guilty of saying, "Well, money isn't everything." Dr. Eikerenkoetter puts it this way. "Never say what money isn't. That expresses indifference toward money. That expresses an indifferent attitude." Not just with money should you not express indifference also with giving your time and talent (paid or unpaid) to be a blessing to others. I believe this place an exclamation points on your authentic success.

I suggest that you use this writing to make an informed decision about what I have called your authentic success a success that encompasses the wholeness of you. I challenge you to research the sources in the bibliography. I believe that from the cellular level to the conscious level of thought, your inner workings will determine how your journey unfolds. Also, I think there is not a personal development self-help book or speaker on the planet that does not emphasize that your life is a manifestation of your thoughts and that there is infinite energy that continually seeks to commune with you. Health, happiness, love, success, and prosperity is yours if you choose to receive it.

MEDITATION and DEEP BREATHING

On my journey to my authentic success, I have discovered that meditation and deep breathing works for me. For example, when I came home after open heart surgery, I had terrible nightmares to the point where my doctors had to prescribe active sleeping and pain medication. I remembered in one of the chapters of my book, I wrote about mindfulness meditation. So, I did a little bit more research and started following the steps of how to do it. Meditating, for me, was difficult at first.

Eventually, the nightmares stopped, and the medication was unnecessary when I started meditating and visualizing good health and happiness before I went to bed. I also perform deep breathing exercises during the day. I believe this has played a significant role in my healing process. I think if you start these repetitive practices, your stress levels will decrease, and your focus on life (conscious awareness) will increase. I use meditation apps downloaded to my smartphone. These are just a few 'techniques' that you can use as tools for your authentic success.

RIGHT NOW, …

Overall, you have to recognize and use the power of the "I AM" that lives within you. Knowing who you are, taking responsibility for yourself and realizing that you impact the world around you with the power of your thoughts is a step in the right direction towards your authentic success. Living life on purpose is the key to your overall success. Your good health, happiness, love, success, prosperity, and use of money depend on your constant awareness and conscious thoughts. I will quickly explain and let you get started on your journey. Allow us to begin with health. If you consistently pay attention to what you eat, how you sleep, how your body reacts to specific environments, and the words you say concerning your health have an impact on your biology. Did you know the name of the "I AM" can keep you healthy? If you believe this put your hands on any area of discomfort, you have been challenged within your body, say this aloud and mean it … *Right now, I AM Healthy and Whole! I see myself as a healthy person because of the presence of the "I AM" that lives in me?* When you do this, make sure you use the techniques mentioned above.

Your happiness is yours and yours only. I believe that you cannot depend on anyone else to make you happy. Your spouse, significant other, pastor, dog, etc. Should not carry the burden of making you happy. Once you give that responsibility or authority to something or someone else you are setting yourself up for a letdown. With a smile on your face whenever you pass a mirror and see yourself say *I AM happy!* Say it with expression and feeling remember the presence of the "I AM" that lives in you makes you happy.

Even on a sad occasion when you do not feel like smiling smile anyway, it will trick your subconscious, and that sad feeling program will not run. That terrible feeling can cause you to eat the wrong things, say something you might regret, cause your blood pressure to increase, or trigger pain in your body. So, let the joy of having the presence and power of the infinite in you be your strength!

Being seeing and feeling love is essential to your success. This is such a sensitive area I will not linger on it. However, the same rules that I stated for happiness apply to love. What I will add is that the goals that you have set for your success have to be met with love. You have to love what you are doing or attempting to do. That love will project to everything and everyone around you and will come back to you in-kind. Using the techniques as mentioned earlier hug yourself and say *the presence of the "I AM" in me loves me unconditionally I AM loved, and I Am love!!*

As stated at the beginning of this book, your authentic success is personal to you. Others may see a janitor cleaning up an office but do not know that you are the owner of the cleaning company. That success belongs to you. Some may see you serving in a restaurant without knowing that you are the Chef in charge. That success is authentic to you. Still, you may be viewed as just a store clerk but unknown to others you are a millionaire entrepreneur who's helping out in one of your many stores. The "world mind" may see a janitor, cook, and store clerk to the outside world that may be a fact, but it is not the truth about you. Your success is your truth. The law of mind affirms this principle in the book of Joshua, chapter 1 verse 8 *Study this Book of Instruction continually. Meditate on it day and night so you will be sure to obey everything written in it. Only then will you prosper and succeed in all you do.*

I said before, if you cannot read or comprehend how can one read or understand the esoteric principles and laws found in ancient text. I warn you if you depend on a person to read for you. You have given your creative authority to another, and it could lead to personal disappointment later in your life. Say this, *right now, I believe I am successful in all the good that I desire to do because the presence of the "I AM" lives in me.*

Prosperity in the context of your authentic success has to be internal and external One must first have to consciously believe that he or she deserves to be prosperous. It is not just for the preachers, certain ethnic groups or entertainers it is for you right here and right now. Prosperity is a state of mind. In the salutation of an ancient letter written in the book of Third John Chapter 1 verse 2, *Beloved, I pray you to prosper concerning all things and to be in good health, just as your soul prospers.* The soul, the energy that is you must first see itself as having a prosperous feeling. First, let me show you that your energy (soul) is active. I want you to look at this phrase and read it in your mind with the feeling I am Prosperous! Say it to yourself again yell it out in your mind I am Prosperous!

Now, did you hear your voice even though your mouth did not move? Now I want you to close your eyes and think of waves crashing on the shore of a sandy beach. Did you hear and see the beach? Your (energy) soul just traveled somewhere your body may not have gone. Your soul allowed you to travel back in time to see and feel a peaceful memory. I said that to say the kingdom of the infinite which lives in you has given you the power to create your prosperity. So as your soul prospers, thus will your body manifest success into the tangible world.

I am wealthy. I believe money is not evil in itself. Just like wisdom is described as a beautiful lady who is more precious than silver or gold. If there was a personification for money, I believe it would be friendly, adventurous, sensitive, and kind but willing to take the risk. I think money, as it relates to your authentic success, follows the principles of these scriptures Romans Chapter 4, and Verse 17, *As it is written: "I have made you a father of many nations." He is our father in the presence of God, in whom he believed, the God who gives life to the dead and calls into being what does not yet exist.* Just as the presence of the "I AM" abided in Abraham that same presence abides in you and gives you the ability to manifest your thoughts into physical reality. So, what are your right now beliefs about money? If you say you do not need it, the money will see you as being unfriendly, and if you have it, the funds will gradually shy away from you. If you say that you do not need money but are in financial crisis, the money will stay away from you because it is not sure how you feel about it. Having money will allow you to do the good that you desire. If you want to buy a fancy car, the salesperson and his or her family will be blessed with a commission. If you're going to buy a big home, the realtor and his or her family are blessed If you want to go on vacation, those people who are working at the hotel will be able to maintain their household budget. That is the adventurous side of money. The kind side of money is that money wants to be used not spent. When money is used correctly and wisely it can circulate back to you to be used again because it (money) sees you as a friend.

However, if you believe in your mind that you do not deserve money or poverty and struggle is your lot in life, you fail to use the free gift that the "I AM" has placed in you. Deuteronomy Chapter 8 and Verse 18 reads: But *remember that it is the LORD your God who gives you the power to gain wealth, to confirm His covenant that He swore to your fathers, as it is this day.* So, the ability to achieve financial wealth is present in you. It is not just for the "megachurch pastors," the drug dealers, including the pharmaceutical companies, the banks, insurance corporations, etc. The ability to be wealthy is equally divided among every human being the key is your faith and believing that you have the power.

These systems use a lot of money to keep you from realizing who you really are. The teacher we call Jesus whole mission was to let people know the kingdom of the infinite abides in you. However, religious folk believes that their so-called shepherds and modern-day prophets are the only ones who have direct access to the "I AM." This is not true. Use the presence of God in you to unveil this passage of scripture from Luke Chapter 16, Verse 16, *The Law and the Prophets were proclaimed until John. Since that*

JW Rucker Jr.

time, the gospel of the kingdom of God is being preached, and everyone is forcing his way into it. You have the power to set yourself financially free. Your friend money is waiting for you to use it for the good that you desire.

Aligning your conscious thoughts with the presence of the "I AM" in you will allow you to see and recognize the divinity of you. The divine you are healthy, happy, loving, and prosperous. The divine you is the truth of you. You have to believe that by faith. Right now, I pray that you understand the navigation process of your journey to authentic success.

If you are reading this and have yet to embark on your journey right now is an excellent time to start. Your right now thoughts can override those old thoughts and perceptions that hang out in your subconscious mind, and you can literally start a new life right now. It will not be easy; the work will be hard. Prayer and meditation are needed at least three times a day to enforce your belief about the new you into your spirit.

Every thought should be focused on the positive. Read and understand the principles of ancient text. The presence of the infinite in you will help you discern fact from truth. I want to conclude this volume with an affirmative meditation/prayer inspired by Dr. Eikerenkoetter. Say these words to yourself at least three times a day read this book and other positive materials over and over until unbelief and fear are conquered

I enter the Kingdom of Heaven that is in me through Jesus, who is the way, truth, and life. I see my divine-self having and doing the good that I desire here in the land of the living. I believe right now, I am healthy, happy, successful, and prosperous. God has made me able to be wealthy, to be a lender and not a borrower. I believe I see thousands of dollars in my hands right now. I am pulling thousands of dollars in checks made out to me right now out of my mailbox. I see multiple money deposits in my bank account right now. I will use my money to do the good that I desire. I believe that my money will circulate through the land and return back to me. This is the good fruit that I want to bare. Starting right now. Thank you, Infinite father, for your presence. Thank you for what I have right now. Thank you for the love you share with me.

END

ABOUT THE AUTHOR

JW Rucker Jr. has helped others live their life on purpose for the past twenty years. after a life-changing medical event his background in education and leadership has helped him become a successful entrepreneur. and motivator. Through personal outreach, he has motivated others who are facing life-changing medical challenges.

He has recently started Walking on Water Outreach Ministries where he uses the principles of science, psychology and spiritual dynamics as a guiding light to align the lives of his audience. He continues to share his message of authentic success through his ministry and podcast.

Contact the author through Walking on Water Outreach Ministries
http://www.WOWMINS.org

Bibliography

Allen, James. *As a Man Thinketh: The Bestselling Classic That Inspired "The Secret"*. New York? Tribeca Books, 2011.

BERNAY, EDWARD. *PROPAGANDA*. S.l.: LULU COM, 2016.

Campbell, Mike. "Names and Personal Identity." Behind the Name. Accessed March 29, 2018. https://www.behindthename.com/articles/3.

Caprino, Kathy. "The Most Common (And Harmful) Ways People Sabotage Their Own Success." Forbes.com, April 2, 2014. https://www.forbes.com/sites/kathycaprino/2014/04/02/the-most-comm...-and-harmful-ways-people-sabotage-their-own-success/#18e6fc0d6f3c.

Chan, Amanda L. "9 Scientifically-Backed Ways To Stop Worrying." The Huffington Post, December 7, 2017. https://www.huffingtonpost.com/2013/10/01/stop-worrying-anxiety-cycle_n_4002914.html.

ChoMay, Adrian, Meredith WadmanMar, Sean Reilly, E&E NewsMar, Jocelyn KaiserMar, Dennis NormileMar, and Benjamin Storrow. "Stephen Hawking's (Almost) Last Paper: Putting an End to the Beginning of the Universe." Science, May 3, 2018. https://www.sciencemag.org/news/2018/05/stephen-hawking-s-almost-last-paper-putting-end-beginning-universe.

Cialdini, Robert B. *Influence: the Psychology of Persuasion*. New York, NY: Collins, n.d.

Crosby, Dan. "Chapter 7: Relating to Others." In *Psychological Triggers: How to Use the Dark Secret Techniques of Psychology to Control, Influence, Persuade and Manipulate Anyone*, 425–26. Make Profits Easy LLC, 2016.

Crosby, Dan. *Psychological Triggers: How to Use the Dark Secret Techniques of Psychology to Control, Influence, Persuade and Manipulate Anyone.* CreateSpace Independent Publishing Platform, 2016.

Dyer, J. "Two Major Psy Ops Documents You Must Read." Truthstream Media, February 25, 2017. http://truthstreammedia.com/2015/05/12/two-major-psy-ops-documents-you-must-read/.

Eikerenkoetter, Frederick. *Rev. Ike's Secrets for Health, Happiness, and Prosperity--for You! a Science of Living Study Guide.* F. Eikerenkoetter, 1982.

Frate, Sasha. "Re-Programming Your Subconscious Mind: A New Script For Health and Relationships With Dr. Bruce Lipton." Face the Current, May 16, 2019. https://facethecurrent.com/bruce-lipton-3/.

Graves, G. "Unlock Your Emotional Intelligence." *TIME*, December 2017.

Hagenston, Richard. *Fabricating Faith: How Christianity Became a Religion Jesus Would Have Rejected.* Salem, OR: Polebridge Press, 2014.

Hardy, Darren. *The Entrepreneur Roller Coaster: Why Now Is the Time to #Jointheride.* Lake Dallas, TX: Success, 2015.

Henrigues, Gregg. "The College Student Mental Health Crisis." Psychology Today, February 15, 2014. https://www.psychologytoday.com/us/blog/theory-knowledge/201402/the-college-student-mental-health-crisis.

Howes, Ryan. "The Definition of Insanity Is..." Psychology Today, July 27, 2009. https://www.psychologytoday.com/us/blog/in-therapy/200907/the-definition-insanity-is.

Johnson, S. C. "Neural Correlates of Self-Reflection." *Brain* 125, no. 8 (2002): 1808–14. https://doi.org/10.1093/brain/awf181.

Kimbro, Dennis Paul. *The Wealth Choice: Success Secrets of Black Millionaires: Featuring the Seven Laws of Wealth*. New York: St. Martin's Griffin, 2014.

Lieberman, David J. *You Can Read Anyone: Never Be Fooled, Lied to, or Taken Advantage of Again*. Kuala Lumpur: YLP Publications, 2012.

Lipton, Bruce H. *The Biology of Belief: Unleashing the Power of Consciousness, Matter & Miracles*. Hay House, Inc., 2016.

Mailonline, Tim Collins For. "Being Rich and Successful Really Is in Your Genes, Study Suggests." Daily Mail Online. Associated Newspapers, July 11, 2018. https://www.dailymail.co.uk/sciencetech/article-5934673/Being-rich-successful-really-genes-study-suggests.html.

Marden, Orison Swett. *Every Man a King: or, Might in Mind Mastery*. Santa Fe, NM: Sun Books, 1997.

Martin, Lauren. "7 Things That Are Worth Fighting For If You Want To Live A Fulfilling Life." Elite Daily, December 17, 2018. https://www.elitedaily.com/life/7-things-that-are-worth-fighting-for-if-you-want-to-live-a-fulfilling-life/589120.

Moran, Gwen. "How To Be Objective When You're Emotionally Invested." Fast Company. Fast Company, December 9, 2014. https://www.fastcompany.com/3039453/how-to-be-objective-when-youre-emotionally-invested.

Moskowitz, Clara. "5 Reasons We May Live in a Multiverse." Space.com, December 7, 2012. https://www.space.com/18811-multiple-universes-5-theories.html.

News, CBS. "What's in a Name? Plenty." CBS News, September 24, 2017. https://www.cbsnews.com/news/whats-in-a-name-plenty/.

Nightingale, Earl. *Earl Nightingale's the Strangest Secret*. Gardners Books, 2007.

Nowack, K. "Beyond Goal Setting to Goal Flourishing." American Psychological Association. American Psychological Association, 2017. https://www.apa.org/pubs/highlights/spotlight/issue-101.

Oaklander, M. "All About Emotions." *Time*, December 2017.

Pagles, Elaine. "The Gnostic Gospels." PBS. Public Broadcasting Service, 1998. https://www.pbs.org/wgbh/frontline/article/gnostic-gospels/.

Platt, Suzy. *Respectfully Quoted: a Dictionary of Quotations*. New York: Barnes & Noble, 1993.

SCOTT, BYRON. *SLAM-DUNK SUCCESS: Leading from Every Position on Life's Court*. S.l.: CENTER ST, 2018.

Shickler, Scott, and Jeff Waller. *The 7 Mindsets to Live Your Ultimate Life: an Unexpected Blueprint for an Extraordinary Life*. Roswell, Georgia? 7 Mindsets Media, 2013.

Southwick, Steven M., George A. Bonanno, Ann S. Masten, Catherine Panter-Brick, and Rachel Yehuda. "Resilience Definitions, Theory, and Challenges: Interdisciplinary Perspectives." *European Journal of Psychotraumatology* 5, no. 1 (2014): 25338. https://doi.org/10.3402/ejpt.v5.25338.

Tannen, Deborah. *The Argument Culture: Stopping America's War of Words*. New York: Ballantine Books, 2006.

"The 5th Gate – Prayer | Meditation | Decrees." The Golden Pathway. Summit Publications, September 23, 2017. https://thegoldenpathway.org/twelve-gates/gate-number-5/.

The Business of Disease. Unknown: Dreamspell Productions, 2014.

They Want You To Be Poor-An Eye Opening Interview. YouTube. YouTube, 2019. https://www.youtube.com/watch?v=m6pWEzkbnDE&t=122s.

Tracy, Brian. "The Power of Your Subconscious Mind | Brian Tracy." Brian Tracy's Self Improvement & Professional

Development Blog. Brian Tracy International Publisher Logo, December 12, 2018. https://www.briantracy.com/blog/personal-success/understanding-your-subconscious-mind/.

Warren, John. "Research Shows a Technique to Offset the Worry of Waiting." EurekAlert! Accessed March 28, 2019. https://www.eurekalert.org/pub_releases/2017-12/uoc--rsa120417.php.

"What Is Repentance? Biblical Definition and Meaning." Bible Study Tools. Accessed April 21, 2018. https://www.biblestudytools.com/dictionary/repentance/.

Wilson, Willie F. *Releasing the Power within through Spiritual Dynamics: the Genius of Jesus Revealed*. House of Knowledge, 2000.

www.ingramcontent.com/pod-product-compliance
Lightning Source LLC
Chambersburg PA
CBHW071418040426
42445CB00012BA/1210